FORTS OF THE NORTHERN PLAINS

A Guide to Military and Civilian
Posts of the Plains Indian Wars

JEFF BARNES

University of Nebraska Press | Lincoln

The University of Nebraska Press is part of a land-grant institution with campuses and programs on the past, present, and future homelands of the Pawnee, Ponca, Otoe-Missouria, Omaha, Dakota, Lakota, Kaw, Cheyenne, and Arapaho Peoples, as well as those of the relocated Ho-Chunk, Sac and Fox, and Iowa Peoples.

The color photography and expanded geographical coverage of this book were made possible by the Ronald K. and Judith M. Stolz Parks Publishing Fund established at the Nebraska State Historical Society Foundation, and use of this Fund for this purpose is made in memory of Wayne Kemper Parks (1909–1995) and Hazel Virginia Hill Parks (1911–1991), lifelong Nebraskans who were born on Madison County farms, were married on March 19, 1930, and were farmers in Madison and Pierce Counties.

Library of Congress Cataloging-in-Publication Data
Names: Barnes, Jeff, 1958– author.
Title: Forts of the Northern Plains: a guide to military and civilian posts of the Plains Indian Wars / Jeff Barnes.
Other titles: Guide to military and civilian posts of the Plains Indian Wars
Description: Expanded edition. | Lincoln: University of Nebraska Press, [2024] | Includes bibliographical references.
Identifiers: LCCN 2023049003
ISBN 9781496235053 (paperback)
ISBN 9781496239969 (epub)
ISBN 9781496239976 (pdf)
Subjects: LCSH: Indians of North America—Wars—1866-1895—Guidebooks. | Indians of North America—Wars—Great Plains—Guidebooks. | Fortification—Great Plains—Guidebooks. | Great Plains—Guidebooks. | BISAC: HISTORY / United States / State & Local / Midwest (IA, IL, IN, KS, MI, MN, MO, ND, NE, OH, SD, WI) | HISTORY / Military / Fortifications
Classification: LCC E83.866 .B37 2024 | DDC 917.80402—dc23/eng/20240215
LC record available at https://lccn.loc.gov/2023049003

Set in Minion Pro by A. Shahan.

To Lyla Belle

CONTENTS

25 FORTS OF MINNESOTA

65 FORTS OF MONTANA

189 FORTS OF WYOMING

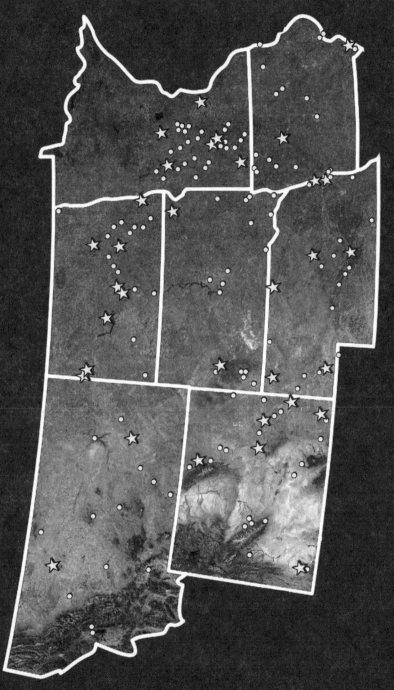

1. Forts of the Northern Plains

INTRODUCTION

When I wrote the first edition of *Forts of the Northern Plains* in 2008, it was intended as a snapshot of the military post sites at that point in time. Most of these locations are open and visible to the public, but changes in ownership, budget cutbacks, even floods and droughts impact the ability to visit them. The very first fort I visited back in 2005—Fort Ridgely in Minnesota—had an active visitor center with a museum and gift shop; now the park is an unmanned site with only a self-guided tour. Fort Custer's large historical marker was moved from its original fort site to the museum in Hardin, Montana. Other sites have altered hours and even seasons of operation. After more than fifteen years, I thought it was time for a new snapshot.

For the first edition, I covered only the sites referred to as "forts," resulting in fifty featured locations. For this edition, I expanded the listing to the smaller camps, posts, and detachments of the government, civilian stockades built for protection, and even trading posts that temporarily had military occupation. Consistent with the first edition, there needed to be something marking the site—be it a state park or a stone—to indicate the post was there.

This resulted in more than 150 marked sites for this guide, a seemingly large number which is but a portion of the military and civilian posts built here on the Plains. It's important to remember that the U.S. Army or civilian communities intended these posts to exist only as long as needed, be it a few days, weeks, months, or years. It's wonderful that many of these were marked at all, and the fact that some are still active military posts is remarkable.

I've updated the guide to include a rating system for the sites, based around amenities and the time you could invest in each. For example, the one-star Fort Robinson in Iowa is a simple marker on the side of a rural highway, but the five-star Fort Robinson in Nebraska has historical markers and original buildings, lodging, a restaurant, two museums, activities, and dramatic scenery. I give special attention to these staffed sites, seeing them as "base camps" for the exploration of other posts in the area, or as the best sites to take in if traveling with a family or on a pressed schedule. A few sites have no stars—they have markers, but their location on private property or their remoteness makes it likely you won't get to see them.

Those fascinated by this history really don't care if there is a park ranger, museum, detailed marker, or even a road waiting for them, though. It's sometimes enough just to stand in an open field and imagine a long-gone parade ground and barracks with scores, sometimes hundreds of men covering these grounds. The remoteness has a benefit in that you'll often find the scenery in much the same state as when the troops first arrived.

A word about tribal designations of the Northern Plains: many of the Native American peoples of the region are reclaiming their original names, such as Ojibwe rather than Chippewa. Recognizing that this is an evolving process, that some tribes' incorporated names aren't the same as their old names, and that I am writing for context and from history, I generally use both names on first reference but try to continue using their current designations.

Finally, an advisory that the Northern Plains *is* an enormous area with weather conditions that can change in minutes. Also, due to the recent pandemic and economic conditions, hours of operation on many of the staffed sites fluctuate as well. I've been to a fort during publicized hours, only to find it was closed to the public that day because of school groups. While I do share the official hours of operation at the staffed sites, it's always a good idea to call ahead to make sure they are open.

I hope you enjoy the history, the landscape, and the people you encounter as you visit these sites. Happy trails!

SITE RANKING SYSTEM

A ranking system with stars is provided for travelers to give an idea of the time needed for a visit and the amenities available. This may be useful for those on a tight traveling schedule or traveling with a partner or family member with no interest in taking *another* detour to visit an historical marker.

★★★★★ Developed, staffed site with original or restored buildings and traveler accommodations, including museums, amenities, and family activities. More than three hours for visitation.

★★★★ Same as above, but without lodging or dining accommodations. Two hours or more for visitation.

★★★ Undeveloped site with original buildings, limited staff, and amenities, but these may be offered nearby. Oriented to adults more than families. One hour for visitation.

★★ Undeveloped site with no staff, but original building or interpretive historical marker present. Limited amenities, such as picnic area or restrooms. Half-hour or less for visitation.

★ Limited historical marker only with no amenities. Less than five minutes for visitation.

☆ Simple place marker without interpretation, or historical marker in remote location with difficult or no public access.

FORTS OF THE NORTHERN PLAINS

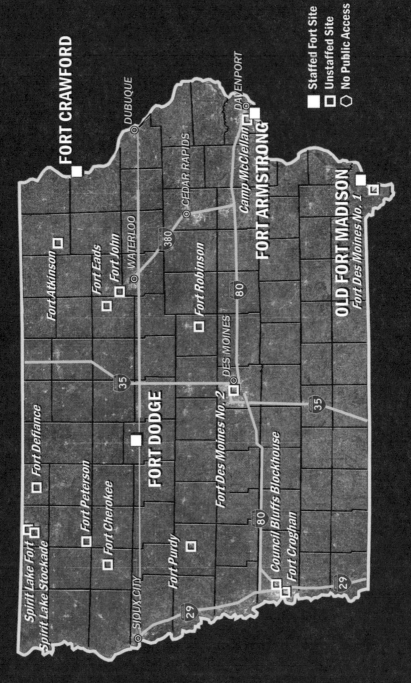

FORT CRAWFORD

DUBUQUE

CEDAR RAPIDS

DAVENPORT

Camp McClellan

FORT ARMSTRONG

WATERLOO

Fort Eads

Fort John

380

Fort Robinson

Fort Atkinson

OLD FORT MADISON

Fort Des Moines No. 1

80

DES MOINES

35

FORT DODGE

Fort Des Moines No. 2

Fort Defiance

Fort Peterson

Fort Cherokee

35

Spirit Lake Fort

Spirit Lake Stockade

Fort Purdy

Council Bluffs Blockhouse

Fort Croghan

80

SIOUX CITY

29

29

■ Staffed Fort Site

◻ Unstaffed Site

⬡ No Public Access

2. Forts of Iowa

FORTS OF IOWA

When the U.S. government began its expansion into today's eastern Iowa, the major tribes were the Sauk (or Sac), the Meskwaki (Fox), Ho-Chunk (Winnebago) and the Dakota Sioux. Beginning with Fort Madison on the Mississippi in 1808, the early U.S. forts encouraged the tribes to trade with Americans, rather than the British, while giving the government a foothold in the territory to protect the eventual settlement by Euro-Americans.

The United States signed treaties with the native tribes, sometimes compelled by war and often involving the cession of land. The forts on the eastern bank of the Mississippi—including Fort Crawford in Wisconsin and Fort Armstrong in Illinois—helped monitor and enforce the treaties in the Iowa territory. As settlement increased and pushed west and north in the 1850s, increasing conflict with the Dakota brought both federal posts like Fort Dodge as well as civilian defenses.

Today, historical markers represent the majority of Iowa's military posts. Only Fort Atkinson retains original buildings at their original site, while both Fort Madison and Fort Dodge were rebuilt as tourist attractions by their namesake cities. An original building of Fort Dodge still stands, albeit not at its original location.

1. Gen. Stephen Watts Kearny, the namesake of Camp Kearny, also provided the name for two Fort Kearnys in Nebraska and the alternatively spelled city of Kearney, Nebraska. Courtesy Missouri History Museum.

Camp Kearny/Council Bluffs Blockhouse   ★

U.S. Dragoons built an oak-log blockhouse at the foot of bluffs overlooking the Missouri River in August 1837 to maintain peace between the Pottawattamie and Dakota of the area. The blockhouse had no formal name but was sometimes referred to as Camp Kearny in dispatches, since its construction was ordered by Col. Stephen W. Kearny, then commander of Fort Leavenworth downstream. The fort recalled troops from the quiet post in November, opening the way for Jesuit priest Father Pierre Jean de Smet to establish a mission there the following year, and operating it through 1841. In 1971 the Historical Society of Pottawattamie County placed a boulder to commemorate the blockhouse near the site.

Location: Marker is at the southwest corner of East Pierce and Franklin Avenues in Council Bluffs; a similar marker to Father de Smet is at the east end of the block. **GPS:** 41.264184°, -95.840386°.

Camp McClellan   ★

Camp McClellan (named for Union Gen. George B. McClellan) was the largest of five Davenport-area Union army camps in 1861. During the Civil War, more than half of the state's eighty thousand volunteers passed through here for mustering and training. Overlooking the Mississippi River, the post grew in December 1863 with a stockade built to confine Winnebago (Ho-Chunk) participating in the Dakota Outbreak in Minnesota the previous year. The stockade itself was called Camp Kearney, and Indians were apparently kept there throughout the Civil War.

A portion of Camp McClellan's 300-plus acres today makes up Lindsay Park, where the local chapter of the Daughters of the American Revolution (DAR) dedicated a boulder marker to the camp. The shaded park is in two historic districts with a sizable number of Civil War–era homes and buildings remaining, making for a pleasant stop.

Location: Lindsay Park is in east Davenport, on the north side of the East River Drive. Turn north from the drive onto Mound Street, go east on East

Eleventh Street for about two-tenths of a mile to find the Camp McClellan boulder on the right. **GPS**: 41.530980°, -90.542865°.

Fort Armstrong

Although not located in a Northern Plains state, the proximity of Rock Island to the Mississippi River and the placement of Fort Armstrong there had tremendous effect on the Iowa and Minnesota territories.

2. The Fort Armstrong blockhouse replica memorializes the federal government's first installation on Rock Island, now known as Arsenal Island and home of the Rock Island Arsenal.

For generations, the Sauk and Meskwaki (Sac and Fox) used the island as a summer retreat, enjoying the wild game, fishing, fruit, and berries there. Lt. Zebulon Pike first noted the "big island" when sent by Thomas Jefferson in 1805 to explore the river and identify possible fort sites; Congress followed up four years later and reserved the now-named "Rock Island" as a federal military reserve. After the War of 1812, in which several forts were lost to the British, the United States advanced its fort plans for the frontier and began work on a Rock Island fort in 1816.

Naming it for U.S. Secretary of War John Armstrong, the Army built the fort to discourage British-Canadian and French-Canadian traders from operating in U.S. lands and to protect settlers there. Pressures of settlement on the indigenous Sauk eventually led to the 1832 war with Black Hawk, chief of the tribe. During the war, troops carrying cholera arrived at Fort Armstrong and caused an epidemic among soldiers, settlers, and Indians in the area. Nearly two hundred died and were buried on Rock Island.

3. Portrait of Black Hawk by George Catlin, 1832. Courtesy Smithsonian American Art Museum.

After the signing of a treaty at Fort Armstrong and the temporary imprisonment of Black Hawk, his sons, and other warriors there in 1832, the government removed the Sauk from Illinois into Iowa. Since the so-called "Indian problem" was gone, the troops abandoned Fort Armstrong in 1836. The government had little use for the island until the Civil War, when the island became a prison for roughly 12,400 captured Confederate soldiers. After the war, the Army began ordnance manufacturing as the Rock Island Arsenal and renamed the island "Arsenal Island." The manufacturing continues today.

A three-story replica of the Fort Armstrong blockhouse was built for the fort's centennial in 1916. Now more than a century old itself, the blockhouse stands as a memorial to one of the first forts built west of the Mississippi (or, from its perspective, *on* the Mississippi).

Location: The blockhouse replica is on the public access west end of Arsenal Island. To reach it from Davenport and East 2nd Street, cross the Mississippi River on the double-decked Arsenal Bridge; after crossing, you'll find yourself on Fort Armstrong Road with the blockhouse and park on your right. **GPS:** 41.516314°, -90.565640°.

A visit to the historic **Rock Island Arsenal Museum** is a must, covering the U.S. Army's presence on the island from Fort Armstrong through the military manufacturing of today. Opened in 1905, it is the second-oldest U.S. Army museum in the country (West Point's museum opened in 1857) and features an outstanding collection of more than 1,200 unique firearms. Since the museum is on an active military post, you'll need to have legal ID to enter the grounds from the Moline (Illinois) Gate Visitor Center, and foreign nationals are not permitted unless on official business. The visitor center provides directions to the museum.

Hours: Open Tuesday through Saturday, noon to 4:00 p.m.; closed federal holidays and the day after Thanksgiving.

Admission: Free

Phone: (309) 782-5021

Email: riamuseum@army.mil

Website: arsenalhistoricalsociety.org

While on post, you can visit the **Mississippi River Visitor Center** which has an historical marker for Fort Armstrong. The island also includes the **Davenport House,** home of homesteader, businessman, and mediator George Davenport, who arrived with the army in 1816 as an agent of the American Fur Company. He soon established strong connections with the Sauk and

4. The Rock Island Arsenal Museum.

helped negotiate peace during the Black Hawk War. The substantial home he built here in the 1830s became the foundation for the Quad Cities of Illinois's Rock Island and Moline and Iowa's Bettendorf and namesake Davenport.

Hours: Open Thursday through Saturday, noon to 4:00 p.m.

Admission: Fee charged

Website: davenporthouse.org

Finally, the **Rock Island National Cemetery** includes among its noted interments Bvt. Brig. Gen. Thomas Jackson Rodman. The inventor and designer of several types of heavy cannon during the Civil War, he's especially known for the famed Rodman guns, which were the primary coastal defense weapons during that war and the rest of the century.

Fort Atkinson ★★

Although mostly in a state of "preserved ruins," Fort Atkinson is the only fort site in Iowa with original buildings at their original locations. This northeast Iowa fortification began as a U.S. Army camp in 1840 as a buffer between the Dakota Sioux and the Sauk and Meskwaki, but then served to protect the Ho-Chunk (Winnebago) from other tribes after their forced migration from Wisconsin. Named for department commander Col. Henry Atkinson, the camp was elevated to "fort" status after the construction of substantial buildings using limestone quarried from the adjacent hillside. A company of U.S. Dragoons joined the infantry in 1841 to keep the Ho-Chunk from returning to Wisconsin.

The infantry left in 1845 and the Dragoons joined Col. Stephen W. Kearny in 1846 for the Mexican-American War. Volunteer troops partially manned the post at that time and mounted militia helped move the Ho-Chunk to their Minnesota reservation in 1848, but the fort was completely abandoned the next year.

5. Using locally sourced limestone helped ensure the survival of Fort Atkinson's north barracks, the largest structure on the preserved site.

The War Department sold the fort at public auction in 1855 with the military reservation surveyed and platted to become the town of Fort Atkinson. Many of the buildings were torn down, the salvage used in the town's structures. Citizens of the town, however, called for the preservation of the original buildings around 1900, and in 1921 the state of Iowa acquired part of the fort and established a state preserve in 1968.

Today's **Fort Atkinson State Preserve** contains the buildings and structural remains of the fort, including barracks, cannon houses, and a powder magazine. This is an unstaffed site and information kiosks are available for the self-guided visit; there is a small museum, opened by appointment only through contacting the nearby Volga River State Recreation Area office (below). The best time to visit is during the annual Fort Atkinson Rendezvous, held during the last full weekend of September, featuring life on the frontier in 1840s Iowa, with buck skinners, Dragoons, black-powder shoots, crafts, and demonstrations.

Location: 303 2nd Street NW, Fort Atkinson IA 52144. **GPS:** 43.145737°, -91.939377°.

Hours: Open daily 4:30 a.m. to 10:30 p.m.

Phone: (563) 425-4161 (Volga River State Recreation Area)

Email: Volga_River@dnr.iowa.gov

Fort Cherokee   ★

CHEROKEE, CHEROKEE COUNTY

In 1862 a growing famine among the Dakota of Minnesota and the failure of the U.S. government to make promised annuity payments led the tribe to attack and kill white settlers in their Minnesota River valley homeland. Fears of Minnesota's "Dakota Uprising" spreading to the south compelled the Iowa Northern Border Brigade to build a fort at Cherokee in 1862–63. The fort included a blockhouse, officer's quarters, guardhouse, granary, a well, and stables within its triangular stockade. After the troops abandoned the post, townspeople dismantled it for its lumber and the blockhouse was taken apart and rebuilt in Cherokee as a home, later destroyed by fire. In 1925 the local Webster School placed a small plaque on a block of granite at the site to commemorate Fort Cherokee.

Location: The marker is in a private yard in northeast Cherokee at Riverview and Colony Drive, approximately 2 blocks south of Riverview and State Highway 3. **GPS:** 42.760492°, -95.534856°.

Note: The **Sanford Museum and Planetarium,** located at 117 East Willow Street, Cherokee IA 51012, has a small display on the triangular fort, showing a model and plans for its construction.

Fort Crawford

PRAIRIE DU CHIEN, CRAWFORD COUNTY, WISCONSIN

This fortification on the Mississippi River in Wisconsin was important to the settlers of northeast Iowa and their relationships with the tribes of the region. The federal government constructed Fort Crawford on St. Feriole Island in 1816 due to fears of British-Canadians continuing to exert trade influence over the Indians of the Upper Mississippi. Named for U.S. Secretary of War William H. Crawford and built on the low east bank of the Mississippi, the timbered Fort Crawford proved convenient for travelers up and down the river or heading east to the Great Lakes. It also kept the peace between the white settlers and the tribes of the area.

The U.S. government conducted negotiations with the native tribes at Fort Crawford, including almost a dozen Indian nations meeting to sign the first Treaty of Prairie du Chien in 1825. Disease and flooding at the site, however, led the War Department to order construction of a new fort in 1829 on a high terrace to the south of the original, this time using locally quarried limestone and locally fired brick. The heavier material and lack of federal funding meant continual delays. Men did not move into the barracks until 1832, and the entire fort was not finished until 1835.

In the meantime, the Black Hawk War began in Illinois and Fort Crawford's troops protected local settlements. After his defeat at the Battle of Bad Axe, Chief Black Hawk surrendered to the fort commander, future U.S. president Col. Zachary Taylor, and was incarcerated here until his transfer to St. Louis. He was escorted by Lt. Jefferson Davis, the future president of the Confederate States of America.

After the government forced the Ho-Chunk, Sauk, Meskwaki, and Pottawattamie from Wisconsin and Illinois to Minnesota and Iowa, the need for the second Fort Crawford dwindled. The army vacillated between a show of troops and no troops at the fort through 1856; it was finally sold by the government in 1868.

The current sites of both the first and second Fort Crawford each bear a structure. The first fort site on St. Feriole Island at the **Villa Louis Historic Site** has a blockhouse reconstruction, while the second on the south side of Prairie du Chien includes the post's former hospital. That building today is the **Fort Crawford Museum**, which tells the story of the fort's history, Prairie du Chien, and the upper Mississippi. An important component of the museum is the story of its first surgeon, William Beaumont, who made significant discoveries in digestive illnesses while at the post.

Location: Fort Crawford Museum, 717 South Beaumont Road, Prairie du Chien WI 53821. **GPS:** 43.042672°, -91.146508°.

Hours: Open daily except Tuesday, May 1 through October 31, 10:00 a.m. to 4:00 p.m. and by appointment.

Admission: Fee charged

Amenities: Gift shop

Phone: (608) 326-6960

Email: pdchistoricalsociety@gmail.org

Website: fortcrawfordmuseum.com

6. The former post hospital survives today as the Fort Crawford Museum in Prairie du Chien.

Fort Croghan ★

COUNCIL BLUFFS, POTTAWATTAMIE COUNTY

U.S. Dragoons from Fort Leavenworth built this temporary post on the Missouri River in 1842 as a protective buffer for the Pottawattamie against the Dakota. Located about 6 miles from the earlier Camp Kearny and Council Bluffs Blockhouse, Fort Croghan (named for Col. George Croghan, a hero of the War of 1812) was hit by spring flooding from the Missouri River, leading troops to abandon it and move to the former Camp Kearny site. When the waters failed to recede, the men returned to Fort Leavenworth.

The Mormons established Council Point here in 1846 to support a river ferry until an 1853 flood again wiped out the site. The church placed a small wooden marker to Council Point which mentions Fort Croghan.

Location: The marker is southwest of Council Bluffs and west of Lake Manawa. Take 24th Street south from I-80, cross Highway 92, and go a half-mile south to the mandatory left on Gifford Road. The marker is about a tenth of a mile further, on the right and within the trees. **GPS:** 41.211058°, -95.878894°.

Fort Defiance ★

ESTHERVILLE, EMMET COUNTY

When a bloodied and barefoot fifteen-year-old boy staggered into Estherville during the Dakota Uprising of 1862, describing the murder of his parents and others, the town joined many communities in building fortifications. The Northern Border Brigade (headed by Capt. William Ingham) built a stockade within the town of four-inch planks and timber from wherever they could find it. Intended to be called Fort Ingham but instead dubbed "Fort Defiance," the post included barracks, officers' quarters, a commissary, a guardhouse, and a well. The garrison remained for the next two years without incident.

Today, Fort Defiance is remembered at three locations in Estherville: a plaque at the original location, a courthouse monument, and the nearby Fort Defiance State Park, which shares the name but has no other connection.

Location: The plaque is on the north side of a single-story brick building at

103 South 6th Street, Estherville IA 51334. The 1911 DAR monument is on the west side of the Emmet County Courthouse at 114 North 6th Street, Estherville IA 51334. **GPS**: Fort: 43.400825°, -94.836855°; Monument: 43.403393°, -94.836435°.

Fort Des Moines No. 1 ★

MONTROSE, LEE COUNTY

Built 11 miles north of the mouth of the Des Moines River on the Mississippi River, this post began as Camp Des Moines in 1834 to supervise the government's removal of the Sauk and Meskwaki to Iowa after the Treaty of Fort Armstrong. Lt. Col. Stephen W. Kearny established the camp, which was upgraded to "Fort" Des Moines in 1835 to indicate permanence. Peaceful settlement allowed the troops to abandon the fort two years later, however, and the town of Montrose soon developed at the site. A small boulder with a plaque, joined by a flag and information panels, overlooks the Mississippi and marks the fort today.

Location: The boulder is at the end of Main Street in Montrose, between the railroad tracks and the river. **GPS**: 40.532745°, -91.413749°.

Fort Des Moines No. 2 ★

DES MOINES, POLK COUNTY

With the rush of settlers into Iowa Territory, U.S. Dragoons established a post in 1843 to prevent the overrun of the Sauk and Meskwaki reservation. They selected a site at the confluence of the Des Moines and Raccoon Rivers and the War Department revived the name Fort Des Moines for it. In 1846 U.S. Army troops escorted the tribes to a new reservation in Missouri, while remaining troops from the fort left to fight in the Mexican-American War. Settlers quickly swooped in and established the town of Fort Des Moines, shortening it to Des Moines in 1857 when it became the capital of Iowa. The fort site today includes a period log cabin and historical monument.

Location: The fort site is the near south side of downtown Des Moines, at the north end of the baseball stadium's parking lot. Next to the hiking-

7. The site of the second Fort Des Moines is marked with a cabin built during the same era.

biking trail is the large 1908 stone-and-plaque monument from the local DAR chapter; a historical marker and 1840s-era log cabin are located at SW 1st and Elm Streets. **GPS**: 41.581992°, -93.616736°.

Fort Dodge ★ ★ ★ ★

FORT DODGE, WEBSTER COUNTY

Increasing conflict between the Dakota and the settlers of northwest Iowa prompted the U.S. Army to build a fort in the area in 1850. Capt. Samuel Woods of the 6th Infantry established Fort Clarke (named for regimental commander Col. Newman S. Clarke) on the east bank of the Des Moines

8. Although the original Fort Dodge never had walls, a stockade reconstruction represents today's Fort Museum and Frontier Village.

River, opposite the mouth of Lizard Creek, and built a dozen structures before the end of the year; eventually twenty-one buildings covered the fort site.

The troops' wives and families arrived in 1851, a sign of the end of the Indian conflict. They planted gardens for their sustenance and many of the ladies even rode out with the officers on hunting trips. In the fall of 1851 the War Department renamed the fort for Sen. Henry Dodge of Wisconsin, and among its officers was Maj. Lewis A. Armistead, second in command and quartermaster. He went on to greater fame as a brigadier general for the Confederacy and for his martyrized death in leading the last wave of Pickett's Charge at the Battle of Gettysburg.

Troops abandoned the fort in 1853 after they went to Minnesota to help establish Fort Ridgely on the Mississippi. The post's civilian storekeeper, William Williams, bought the buildings and military reservation and platted the new town of Fort Dodge. The fort's buildings disappeared over time, and in 1928 the Fort Dodge chapter of the DAR marked the site of the fort with an historical marker on the northwest side of downtown Fort Dodge.

Although it isn't a reconstruction of Fort Dodge or located at the fort site, an essential visit is the **Fort Museum and Frontier Village**. The stockade part of the museum is a replica of Fort Williams, one of the community defenses

9. The original log quarters of Maj. Lewis A. Armistead were found and restored in Fort Dodge for the fort museum.

built during the Dakota Uprising of 1862, originally built near the Minnesota border. The original log office of Major Armistead is also here—it was sold along with the rest of the fort after its closing and was moved and converted to a private home. During the demolition of that home in the 1960s, workers found the original cabin under layers of resurfacing. It was spared and moved to the museum for restoration to its original appearance. The museum includes many other artifacts from the fort and the Fort Dodge community.

Location: Fort Museum and Frontier Village: 1 Museum Road, Fort Dodge IA 50501. The Fort Dodge marker is at the offices of the Webster County Department of Health Services: 330 1st Avenue N. **GPS:** Museum: 42.488423°, -94.199033°; **Marker:** 42.505616°, -94.192604°.

Hours: Open daily mid-April through mid-October, Monday through Saturday, 10:00 a.m. to 5:00 p.m., Sunday 11:00 a.m. to 5:00 p.m. Museum hours vary in the off-season and weather conditions, so call ahead to confirm.

Admission: Fee charged

Phone: (515) 573-4231

Email: fortmuseumfd@gmail.com

Website: fortmuseumfv.com

Fort Eads ★

CLARKSVILLE, BUTLER COUNTY

Large numbers of Dakota still in the area of north-central Iowa in 1854 disturbed settlers to the point that retired Mexican-American War colonel and then-state school official Abner Eads organized a patrol of mounted volunteers in Cedar Falls to cover the area. When they arrived at Clarksville, a detachment built a small trench-and-breastwork defense they called "Fort Eads." There never was a real threat of attack by the Dakota—in fact, Eads and his un-uniformed "Dragoons" marching through the area caused more fear than the Indians. With the hastily-built fort long since gone, townspeople in 1939 placed a small boulder and plaque to mark the eighty-fifth anniversary of this civilian defense.

Location: The boulder is at the northwest corner of Superior and Adams Streets, west of downtown Clarksville. **GPS:** 42.784775°, -92.671694°.

Fort John ★

JANESVILLE, BREMER COUNTY

Like Fort Eads, Fort John was a civilian defense built during the increasing fears of the Dakota in 1854. Quaker abolitionist John Barrick founded Janesville in 1849, naming the town after his wife Jane. Defenders first named the post Fort Barrick, but apparently renamed it Fort John to fall in with the town's first-name informality.

Fort John saw no action in the Indian Wars, but it did serve as a terminus of sorts on the Underground Railroad. According to local history, a tunnel connecting Janesville's business district, several homes, and Fort John transported runaway slaves to the Cedar River and eventually southern Minnesota. The DAR dedicated a boulder and plaque to Fort John at the north end of the business district in 1912.

Location: Boulder is at the northwest corner of Second and Main Streets in Janesville. **GPS:** 42.647307°, -92.463141°.

Old Fort Madison

FORT MADISON, LEE COUNTY

The first permanent fort on Iowa soil came in 1808 with the construction of Fort Madison on the Mississippi River. Named for U.S. Secretary of State James Madison, the fort was to control the Sauk and Meskwaki and to promote trade with local tribes. Fort Madison was part of the U.S. factory system of forts, where manufactured goods like blankets, knives, hatchets, pots, and pans were sold to the tribes at cost while the tribes brought in furs, lead, feathers, beeswax, and other commodities. This trading proved highly profitable, with Fort Madison among the top three highest-grossing forts in the factory system from 1808 to 1811.

That changed during the War of 1812, when tribes like the Ho-Chunk saw the fort as a violation of treaties. They harassed and attacked Fort Madison to the point where the garrison was short of supplies and reinforcements. Rather than risk winter in those conditions, on September 3, 1813 the troops dug a trench under cover of night from the fort to the river for an escape by boat, setting fire to the fort to keep it and its supplies out of Indian hands. A single chimney stood after the fire, serving as a landmark on the river for years after.

The town of Fort Madison soon sprang up around the fort site. Upon the centennial of Old Fort Madison in 1908, the local DAR chapter erected a lone-chimney monument on the shore of the river at the site of Blockhouse No. 1. In the 1980s, volunteer inmates from the nearby Iowa State Penitentiary helped construct replicas of the fort's major buildings for the city of Fort Madison.

The city continues to operate **Old Fort Madison** to depict life at the fort. The best times to visit are during its special events, including "Muster on the Mississippi" on Memorial Day weekend, with warrior reenactors from history; the Independence Day celebration on July 4, with a recreation of the time period's military ceremony; and "Siege 1812," held during the second weekend in September, with a recreation of life at the fort.

Location: Old Fort Madison: 716 Riverview Drive, Riverview Park, Fort Madison IA 52627. The Lone Chimney monument is at Business U.S. Highway 61 and Fourth Street in Fort Madison. GPS: Old Fort Madison: 40.628647°, -91.311080°; Monument: 40.629741°, -91.304063°.

10. The city-owned Old Fort Madison is a reconstruction near the original fort site on the Mississippi River.

Hours: Open June through August, Wednesday through Sunday, 9:00 a.m. to 5:00 p.m.; open weekends only in May, September, and October, 9:00 a.m. to 5:00 p.m. Closed November through April, with tours by appointment.
Admission: Fee charged
Phone: (319) 372-7700, ext. 201
Website: oldfortmadison.org

Fort Peterson

PETERSON, CLAY COUNTY

Similar in design to Fort Cherokee, the fort at Peterson was triangular and constructed over the winter of 1862 through the spring of 1863. The unusual design no doubt made for cramped quarters for its occupants.

After the fort's eventual abandonment, townspeople helped themselves to the lumber from the fort, while the blockhouse was dismantled and rebuilt on a nearby farm as a home and then as a storage shed; its walnut hand-hewn

11. Howitzers guarding the parade ground of Old Fort Madison.

logs survived and were eventually returned to town for reconstruction near the original fort site.

Location: The blockhouse and a large boulder with a bronze plaque carrying a history of the post stand within a small park at Third and Park Streets in Peterson. **GPS:** 42.918898°, -95.340743°.

Fort Purdy   ★

DENISON, CRAWFORD COUNTY

The strongly built home and grounds of John Purdy overlooking the Boyer River Valley became known as "John Purdy's Fort," or Fort Purdy, during the Indian raids of 1854. The presumed attacks never came, but Fort Purdy did protect the county's records. The DAR erected a granite marker in 1914 at the Crawford County Courthouse in Denison to commemorate Fort Purdy, leading some to conclude that the area was the location of the original fort site. Citizens wanting accuracy later moved the marker to the actual bluff site in northeast Denison.

Location: To reach the marker, start from U.S. Highway 30 in southeast Denison, take 20th Street north, drive north for a little more than a mile until the road veers right and becomes Ridge Road. Take this for another quarter-mile through the residential neighborhood until reaching a church at 1019 Ridge Road—the marker is in the church's front yard, facing the street. **GPS:** 42.030305°, -95.338853°.

Fort Robinson   ★

MARSHALLTOWN, MARSHALL COUNTY

Settlers living among the Meskwaki in 1850 built this fort after tribe members killed some hogs, drove off a few head of stock, and threatened a settler. That settler then burned the Indians' crops in retribution, expecting troops at Fort Dodge to drive the Meskwaki out of the county, but was told the U.S. troops were there only to keep the peace. After a suggestion to either get out of the county or protect themselves, the settlers built a ninety-foot-square stockade on land owned by Abner Robinson. They hid in the fort for about a week without incident, and the federal government soon removed the Meskwaki from the county. The Marshall County Historical Society placed a boulder and plaque near the fort site in 1937 to mark the county's contribution to the Plains Indian Wars.

Location: From the intersection of the Old Lincoln Highway (Business Highway U.S. 30) and Governor Road southeast of Marshalltown, travel south for a little more than a mile—the boulder is on your right, above the ditch. **GPS:** 41.990005°, -92.893409°.

Spirit Lake Fort   ★
and Spirit Lake Stockade   ★

SPIRIT LAKE, DICKINSON COUNTY

After the Spirit Lake Massacre of 1857—in which a band of Santee Sioux killed nearly forty settlers and took others hostage—the community built a fort for protection, including a building of twenty-four by thirty feet, surrounded by a stockade. They included a well within the walls to survive a siege, but no additional attacks came, and they tore down the fort two years later.

The Minnesota Dakota Uprising of 1862 stoked fears of another attack on the Spirit Lake community. Somewhere between twenty-five and forty families hid in the incomplete brick Dickinson County Courthouse, and within a week they began building a stockade. Soldiers arrived at this time to help in the construction, and when it was complete, they occupied it and the settlers returned to their homes. The military continued to occupy the "Spirit Lake Stockade" for the next three years, finally abandoning it in the summer of 1865.

The local DAR chapter placed a marker at the Spirit Lake Fort site in 1912 and at the Spirit Lake Stockade site in 1928.

Location: The stockade marker is at the Dickinson County Courthouse in downtown Spirit Lake, at the southwest corner of U.S. Highway 71 and Hill Avenue, 1807 Hill Avenue. The fort marker is 7 blocks north at St. Mary's Catholic Church, 1005 Hill Avenue. **GPS:** Stockade Marker: 43.422446°, -95.102508°; Fort Marker: 43.429806°, -95.102098°.

12. Boulder and plaque recalls the Spirit Lake Fort, the first fort built by citizens for their defense.

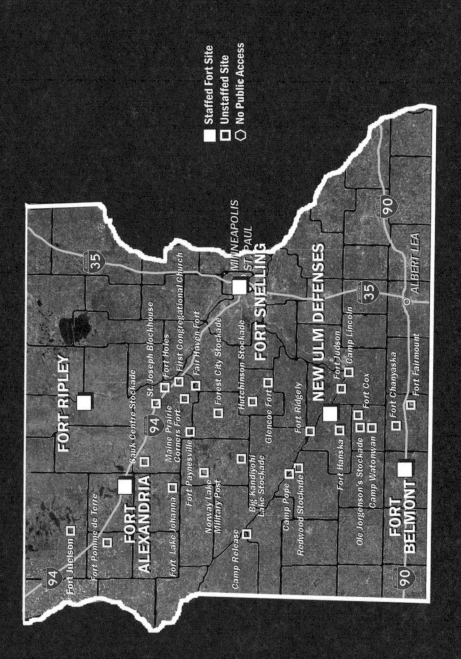

Legend
- ■ Staffed Fort Site
- ☐ Unstaffed Site
- ⬡ No Public Access

FORT RIPLEY

FORT ALEXANDRIA

FORT SNELLING

MINNEAPOLIS
ST. PAUL

NEW ULM DEFENSES

ALBERT LEA

FORT BELMONT

Fort Juelson
Fort Pomme de Terre
Fort Lake Johanna
Norway Lake
Military Post
Camp Release
Sauk Centre Stockade
Maine Prairie
Corners Fort
Fort Paynesville
Big Kandiyohi
Lake Stockade
Redwood Stockade
St. Joseph Blockhouse
Fort Holes
First Congregational Church
Fair Haven Fort
Forest City Stockade
Glencoe Fort
Camp Pope
Hutchinson Stockade
Fort Ridgely
Fort Hanska
Ole Jorgenson's Stockade
Camp Watonwan
Fort Judson
Camp Lincoln
Fort Cox
Fort Chanyaska
Fort Fairmount

3. Forts of Minnesota

FORTS OF MINNESOTA

The major tribes of Minnesota before European arrival were the Dakota (Sioux), Ojibwe (Chippewa), and Ho-Chunk (Winnebago), along with various bands and subgroups within those tribes. Like the first forts of Iowa, Fort Snelling at the confluence of the Minnesota and Mississippi Rivers was built to compel the tribes to trade with Americans and to maintain peace for the eventual immigration of white settlers into native lands.

The federal government built Fort Ripley on the Mississippi in the 1840s to keep peace between the Dakota and Ojibwe; it constructed Fort Ridgely in the 1850s to buffer the Dakota reservation from the white settlement of the Minnesota River valley. All federal posts in the state were woefully unprepared for the Dakota Uprising of 1862 in which hundreds of settlers were killed. As a result, Minnesota citizens went into a defensive mode with scores of civilian forts hastily erected across the state.

Many of these fortification sites are marked today, making for a wonderful tour of Minnesota should you try to see them all. Fort Snelling continues as the oldest fort structure on the Plains, still standing on the cliff overlooking the confluence of the Mississippi and Minnesota Rivers; it's also the most visited historic site in the state. Fort Ridgely is a state property open to the public, although budget cutbacks means it is no longer a staffed site. One of the more interesting "fortification" sites is downtown New Ulm, successfully defended by its citizens in the Dakota Uprising. While the ad hoc walls are long gone, original buildings remain, a walking tour is well marked, and the local museum exceptionally interprets the site and conflict.

Big Kandiyohi Lake Stockade

LAKE LILLIAN, KANDIYOHI COUNTY

U.S. troops established a line of small fortifications after the 1862 Dakota Uprising to keep out both Indians and white settlers until the Minnesota frontier regained its stability. The 8th Minnesota Infantry patrolled and manned these posts, including this stockade built in 1865 on the west shore of Big Kandiyohi Lake. The small fort is remembered via an historical marker at the lake.

Location: Kandiyohi County Park West, 14391 45th Street SE, Lake Lillian MN, 56253 (10 miles south of Willmar). **GPS:** 44.986610°, -94.978397°.

Amenities: Playground, picnic tables, swimming, fishing, boating, and restrooms.

Camp Lincoln

MANKATO, BLUE EARTH COUNTY

Settlers in 1852 originally considered the land at the confluence of the Blue Earth and Minnesota Rivers for a townsite until flood potential deterred them. Ten years later the grounds below Sibley Mound (named for Henry Hastings Sibley, Minnesota's first governor, who once ran a trading post there) became a prison camp named Camp Lincoln for more than three hundred Dakota convicted and condemned for their part in the 1862 uprising. In 1887 the city of Mankato bought the site to create the town's first park.

Sibley Park remains one of Mankato's largest and most popular parks, featuring landscaped gardens, ball fields, restrooms, and playgrounds for visitors. A marker with a history of the park—mentioning Camp Lincoln—is located at the south base of Sibley Mound.

Location: 900 Mound Avenue, Mankato MN 56001. **GPS:** 44.160941°, -94.032836°.

Note: Monuments and markers to the execution of thirty-eight Dakota for their role in the uprising are at Reconciliation Park, near the downtown Blue Earth County Library on South Riverfront Drive at East Main Street.

Camp Pope ★

REDWOOD FALLS, REDWOOD COUNTY

Although the military drove the Dakota from Minnesota west into Lakota lands after the 1862 uprising, former governor Col. Henry H. Sibley pursued them the following year into today's North Dakota. Troops from Fort Snelling

13. Camp Pope marker, placed in 1898.

were organized in April 1863 near Redwood Falls and the Minnesota River in an encampment named for Gen. John Pope, commander of the Department of the Northwest. The Sibley Expedition launched on June 16, 1863. In 1898 the Minnesota Historical Society placed an inscribed granite marker at the site to commemorate Camp Pope.

Location: Taking Highway 101 north from Redwood Falls, and before reaching the Minnesota River, turn left onto River Road and follow it for almost a mile; the marker is on the north side of the road. **GPS:** 44.577756°, -95.111139°.

Camp Release

MONTEVIDEO, LAC QUI PARLE COUNTY

While the Dakota fought Colonel Sibley's troops at the Battle of Wood Lake on September 23, 1862, those friendly to the U.S. government took control of white and mixed-blood hostages held by the Dakota and brought them into their camp. The Dakota, defeated in the battle, returned to gather their families and belongings and retreated into the Dakota Territory. The "friendlies" passed word along to Sibley that he could safely advance, and on September 26, 1862, more than 265 captives were rescued. The site was soon called Camp Release.

On July 4, 1894, the state of Minnesota erected a fifty-one-foot inscribed granite column to commemorate this event, as well as the battles of Redwood Ferry, Fort Ridgley, New Ulm, Birch Coolie, Fort Abercrombie, and Wood Lake. Located about 2 miles west and across the Minnesota River from the town of Montevideo, the Camp Release State Monument was the first property added to the state park system; its wooded pull-off area also includes a state historical marker and interpretive panels.

Location: About 1.5 miles west of Montevideo, at the junction of 445th Avenue with U.S. Highways 212 and 59. **GPS:** 44.933186°, -95.747983°.

14. The fifty-one-foot granite monument of Camp Redwood commemorates the end of the Dakota Uprising as well as the major battles of the conflict.

Camp Watonwan

ST. JAMES, WATONWAN COUNTY

This was one of a line of posts established in 1862 for the protection of settlers. Dakota attacked a small group of settlers near here on April 16, 1863, killing twelve-year-old Christopher Gilbrantson and Pvt. Ole Erickson and wounding five others as they attempted to reach the fort. A small interpretive marker today marks the site of the post.

Location: Take Highway 4 about 6 miles south of St. James and turn left (east) on 420th Street (County Road 7) for 2 miles. The marker is at the intersection with 715th Avenue. **GPS:** 43.877278°, -94.649435°.

Fair Haven Fort

FAIRHAVEN, STEARNS COUNTY

With many of its fighting-age men helping to defend Forest City (see the entry for Forest City Stockade below) in the 1862 uprising, those remaining in Fair Haven built a stockade around an old log hotel to protect women and children while the men worked in the fields during the day. They abandoned the makeshift fort within three weeks and its brief history is commemorated today with a marker in the town park.

Location: Southwest corner of Fair Haven Park, near the intersection of Bridgewater Road and 49th Avenue in Fairhaven (the unincorporated village's name has consolidated from Fair Haven to Fairhaven over the years). **GPS:** 45.321761°, -94.212589°.

First Congregational Church ★

CLEARWATER, WRIGHT COUNTY

New England settlers to Clearwater built a Greek Revival-style Congregational church in 1861 to reflect their "Yankee" heritage. Two years later—after the Dakota Uprising of 1862 and the murder of a local family by Indians in 1863—remaining homesteaders decided to fortify the church since it was the

15. The 1861 First Congregational Church.

largest building in the area. They built a stockade around the building and
provisioned it, but months without an incident brought an end to the scare.
The church has survived after more than 160 years and is in relatively good
shape, but no historical interpretation is at the building.

   Location: First Congregational Church of Clearwater, 405 Bluff Street,
Clearwater MN 55320. **GPS:** 45.419560°, -94.050966°.

Forest City Stockade ★★★

FOREST CITY, MEEKER COUNTY

Hearing of attacks by Dakota Indians, the Home Guard and citizens of Forest City began building a stockade for protection on September 3, 1862. They finished a substantial stockade within twenty-four hours, in time for 240 citizens to take cover when the Dakota began their attack at 3:00 a.m. The walls held off the Dakota, who instead looted the abandoned homesteads before moving on.

In 1976, to commemorate the early history of the community, Meeker County volunteers built a replica of the Forest City stockade near the original site and to the original dimensions. Along with the stockade are buildings for a blacksmith, chapel, doctor's office, general store, gunsmith, land office, and more.

Continually maintained by volunteers, the impressive stockade and village opens its gates twice a year, during a summer rendezvous held every third

16. The Forest City Stockade reconstruction hosts an annual summer rendezvous and a pioneer Christmas for frontier enthusiasts.

weekend in August and for a "Pioneer Christmas" on the first Saturday of each December. Demonstrations, games, and food are part of the fare for each. If you happen to be there outside of these events, there is a granite historical marker at the gates with a brief history of the stockade.

Location: 6 miles north of Litchfield and a half-mile south of Forest City on Minnesota Highway 24.

Phone: (320) 693-6782 or (320) 699-1167

Website: forestcitystockade.org

Fort Alexandria

ALEXANDRIA, DOUGLAS COUNTY

Businessman Solomon Pendergast built a stockade around his Alexandria property during the peak of the 1862 Dakota uprising, making it a store, fort, inn, and even a maternity ward with three children born within its walls during the scare. The 8th Minnesota returned to the stockade a few months after the uprising ended to assure the safe resettlement of the community.

This was a "large" small fort of two acres, with its pentagonal walls holding Pendergast's hotel, officer and soldiers' quarters, stables, granaries, and a

17. A painting of the Fort Alexandria building complex by artist Ada A. Johnson is part of the Runestone Museum collection. Courtesy Runestone Museum.

blacksmith shop. It didn't last long after the resettlement; newspaper accounts lamented the disappearance of the stockade by the late 1860s.

Alexandria's **Runestone Museum** today occupies a portion of the old stockade, and the portion of the museum which is open-air is the Fort Alexandria exhibit. Nine historic buildings, constructed between 1860 and 1910, are within the stockade walls to represent fort life, but are closed in the off-season. The focus of the museum, however, is on the controversial Kensington Rune Stone found nearby and supposedly left by Nordic explorers in the Middle Ages.

Location: Runestone Museum, 206 Broadway Street, Alexandria MN 56308. **GPS:** 45.890449°, 95.377898°.

Hours: Tuesday through Saturday, 10:00 a.m. to 4:00 p.m.

Admission: Varies by season

Phone: (320) 763-3160

Email: director@runestonemuseum.org

Website: runestonemuseum.org

Fort Belmont

JACKSON, JACKSON COUNTY

Settlers of the town of Belmont built a log fortress for their protection in 1864, two years after the Belmont Massacre in which the Dakota killed thirteen settlers. They used the eighteen by twenty-six-foot fort primarily at night and during the summer but were never attacked in its three years of existence. After the Southern Minnesota Railroad crossed the Des Moines River to the south at Jackson in 1879, the community of Belmont soon disappeared. The Jackson County Historical Society cast a bronze marker commemorating the fort site in 1964 for its centennial.

Before that time, in the late 1950s, local interests built **Fort Belmont** to capitalize on southwest Minnesota tourism. The recreated fort also includes a blacksmith shop, sod house, forty-foot lookout tower, a working grist mill, an 1873 farmhouse, a 1902 church, and a museum and gift shop.

Location: Fort Belmont, 217 Belmont Lane, Jackson MN 56143 (southwest of the junction of I-90 and U.S. Highway 71). To reach the historical marker, drive 1.25 miles north on U.S. Highway 71 from the junction to 810th Street, a

18. A replica of the original Fort Belmont serves to commemorate the original civilian defense of the southeast Minnesota community of Belmont.

half-mile west to 535th Avenue, 1 mile north to 820th Street, and .9 miles west to the marker. **GPS**: Fort Belmont Replica: 43.637751°, -95.004784°; Marker: 43.674397°, -95.021909°.

Hours: Open Memorial Day through Labor Day, Monday through Friday 10:00 a.m. to 4:00 p.m., Saturday 9:00 a.m. to 3:00 p.m., Sunday noon to 3:00 p.m.

Admission: Donations accepted

Special Events: Live music festival in July; Pioneer Days, featuring live demonstrations, last weekend in August

Phone: (507) 847-6672

Email: chamber@jacksonmn.com

Fort Chanyaska

One of many forts built during and after the Dakota Uprising in 1862, Fort Chanyaska (named for a nearby lake) was built by the 9th Minnesota Infantry as part of a chain of posts along Minnesota's southern prairie. The local DAR chapter placed a commemorating boulder and plaque near the fort site in 1927.

Location: The boulder is 5.5 miles north of the Welcome exit on I-90 at County Road 27; it lies on the west side of the road, north of Elm Creek and near an entrance to a field and may be difficult to spot in overgrown weeds. **GPS:** 43.760776°, -94.614713°.

Fort Cox

Col. Charles E. Flandrau ordered the construction of this post in the fall of 1862 after the successful defense of New Ulm from raiding Dakota Indians. Capt. E. St. Julien Cox commanded the fort, one of the more uniquely constructed posts with two stories and eight sides as well as breastworks and a moat. Small detachments continued to man the fort through 1865. The Watonwan County Historical Society erected a small historical marker to Fort Cox north of the site in 1966.

Location: Marker is next to the United Methodist Church at 106 Center Avenue North, Madelia MN 56062. **GPS:** 44.052118°, -94.416847°.

Fort Fairmount ★

Fort Fairmount (also known as Fairmont Stockade and Chain-of-Lakes Post) was the southernmost Minnesota fort erected during the Dakota Uprising. The 25th Wisconsin Volunteers built the stockade in September 1862 around the log courthouse, located on a hill overlooking Fairmont and Lake Sisseton. The soldiers used the building as a mess hall during the conflict, and it again served as a temporary courthouse when the county built a new one.

19. One of two markers to Fort Fairmount at the Martin County Courthouse, the site of the stockade.

In 1907 Martin County returned to the site to build the present courthouse, where there are two markers to the fort. Although the town is "Fairmont," both of markers are to Fort "Fairmount."

Location: Martin County Courthouse, 201 Lake Avenue, Fairmont MN 56031. **GPS:** 43.652898°, -94.464708°.

Fort Hanska

HANSKA, BROWN COUNTY

Soldiers of the 9th Minnesota Volunteers built Fort Hanska (or Fort Hill) in the spring of 1863 on a knob above Lake Hanska. Ideally situated for fishing, swimming, and its commanding view of the surrounding countryside, the fort had an eight-foot earthen wall topped with palisades surrounding a log building at its center. Settlers soon built dugouts nearby for the soldiers' protection. Eventually the troops abandoned the fort, and the site became a place for gathering and recreation.

Today's Lake Hanska County Park includes interpretive signage around the old fort site, along with a relocated 1850s log cabin. The nearly eighty-acre site is in the National Register of Historic Places. Four distinct cultures occupied the area throughout history, from pre-historic hunters to European settlers.

Location: About 13 miles south-southwest of New Ulm and about 4 miles west-southwest of Hanska, off County Road 11 about a half-mile north of County Road 6. **GPS:** 44.122901°, -94.554771°.

Hours: Open daily 8:00 a.m. to 10:00 p.m.; campground open from mid-May to late September.

Amenities: Historic sites, swimming, modern camping, fishing, boating, picnic shelters, and restrooms. Handicapped accessible.

Fort Holes

ST. CLOUD, STEARNS COUNTY

Built near the Mississippi River and named for local militia Capt. Samuel Holes, Fort Holes was one of many stockades built in 1862 for protection in the Dakota Uprising. Its construction was such that it couldn't be scaled with a ladder, with walls built three-feet thick at the base and one-and-a-half-feet thick at six or seven feet high. Like most of the other stockades built in the uprising, it was never attacked but did provide a safe haven for refugees from the countryside. Members of St. Cloud State College placed an historical marker to the fort in 1969.

Location: The marker is near the northeast corner of the large parking lot at 4th Avenue South and 9th Street South on the St. Cloud State University Campus. **GPS:** 45.550761°, -94.151666°.

Fort Judson ★

JUDSON, BLUE EARTH COUNTY

Fort Judson was an earthen fort built in 1863 at the town of Judson on the Minnesota River. Sometimes known as the Judson Post or Camp Crisp (due to its construction at Crisp's Store or Crisp's Farm), the fort's perimeter is marked today by grassy berms and large concrete blocks, one of which is marked by a plaque reading simply "Fort Judson 1863."

Location: In Judson, one and a half blocks east of County Road 42 and Judson Fort Road. **GPS:** 44.195767°, -94.192068°.

Fort Juelson ★

UNDERWOOD, OTTER TAIL COUNTY

Fort Juelson was an example of how fast and how far fear could spread on the sparsely populated Plains. The July 14, 1876, edition of the *Fergus Falls Advocate* was the first Minnesota newspaper to print word of Custer's disastrous last stand at the Little Bighorn, almost three weeks after the battle. Seeing wandering Ojibwe in the area sent pioneers fleeing to larger towns, but some decided to stay at their homes and fight, including Underwood farmers and Civil War veterans Capt. Hans Juelson and Berge O. Lee. They selected a hilltop to build a 100-by-120-foot sod fort, which they finished within two weeks. Captain Juelson assembled a 150-man militia and stocked the fort with food and water for an attack that never came.

The local American Legion Post raised a flag at the hilltop in 1974, which today provides a couple of benches and a beautiful view of the countryside.

20. A visit to the site of hilltop defense Fort Juelson requires some hiking.

Location: Travel 2 miles southeast of Underwood on Minnesota Highway 210 and a quarter-mile north on 315th Avenue to parking, an interpretive kiosk, and a trail to the hilltop. **GPS:** 46.272420°, -95.830423°.

Fort Lake Johanna

TERRACE, POPE COUNTY

Another in the line of fortifications built, manned, and never attacked was Fort Lake Johanna, built by the 2nd Minnesota Cavalry in 1865. It was abandoned after several months, and local homesteaders used its logs and wood to build their own homes. Local groups placed a marker to commemorate the fort and the nearby historic Iverson Cabin; the plaque on the marker mentions another marker at the fort site on a ridge to the northeast, which the author was unable to locate.

Location: The marker is about 7 miles north of Sunburg on Minnesota Highway 104 at a scenic overlook. **GPS:** 45.445043°, -95.254426°.

Fort Paynesville

PAYNESVILLE, STEARNS COUNTY

During the 1862 Dakota uprising, the Home Guard of Paynesville built a fort using the town's school and Methodist Church, adding sod, dirt, and timber for its walls. Militia from St. Cloud found the fort overcrowded and falling apart; they moved the occupants to other towns, whereupon the Dakota burned the fort and the whole village. Companies of the 25th Wisconsin built a more substantial fort at the site in October 1862, and troops used it through May 1864.

Location: There is no historical marker for the fort, but an unmarked concrete post can be found at the northeast corner of West Main Street and Business Highway 23 West in Paynesville (920 West Main Street) indicating one of its corners. **GPS:** 45.376715°, -94.729087°.

Fort Ridgely ★★★

FAIRFAX, NICOLLET COUNTY

Settlers poured into the Minnesota River valley after the establishment of the Dakota reservation in the 1850s, and in 1853 the War Department built Fort Ridgely between the southern border of the reservation and the German settlement of New Ulm. Fort Ridgely (named for three men sharing the same last name who died in the Mexican-American War) was built to keep the peace, rather than as a defensive position. Walls weren't necessary since the fort was well-manned and relationships with the Dakota were good.

All of that changed in 1862. After most of the fort's trained troops left to fight for the Union in the Civil War, Dakota and U.S. relations deteriorated due to an inadequate reservation system, wartime economics, violations of treaties, and a growing famine among the Indians.

21. The rebuilt commissary and 1896 granite monument are the most visible signs of Fort Ridgely, while archaeological excavations in 1935 revealed the foundations of eight buildings.

On August 20 about four hundred Dakota attacked the open and under-manned Fort Ridgely and its 180 defenders. U.S. troops used five cannons to drive the Dakota back after a five-hour fight, but a second attack came two days later, with the Dakota doubling their number. Fort defenders fired their cannons again, this time blowing up the fort stables, which gave cover to the Dakota and forced them to withdraw. In the two battles, the Dakota killed only three soldiers and in turn lost as many as a hundred warriors. There were no further attacks on Fort Ridgely, one of the few U.S. posts attacked during the Plains Indian Wars.

After the federal government removed the Dakota from Minnesota, troops abandoned Fort Ridgely in 1867 and local settlers soon occupied some of the buildings and pillaged the rest for construction materials. The state of Minnesota purchased a portion of the original site in 1896 and in that same year erected a large red granite monument in honor of the fort's defenders. The fort site became a memorial park in 1911, and after archeological work commenced in 1936, the rebuilt stone commissary was developed as a museum.

Located in Fort Ridgely State Park, 6 miles south of Fairfax and overlooking the Minnesota River, **Fort Ridgely Historic Site** continues under the ownership of the Minnesota Historical Society. There is a self-guided walking tour among the stone ruins and massive granite monument of the historic fort. The largest remaining building—the commissary—was the visitor center and museum for the fort until budget cutbacks. Stone foundations indicate the sites of original buildings, each with an interpretive marker telling of the building and its role at the fort.

To the east is the fort cemetery, located between the site and the state park's golf course. The cemetery contains the final resting place of several well-known participants of the Dakota War, including Capt. John S. Marsh, the fort's commander who drowned in the Minnesota River while attempting to escape from Indian attack at the Lower Sioux Agency, and Eliza Muller, the wife of the post's surgeon. Mrs. Muller was nicknamed as the "Clara Barton of the Minnesota Frontier" for her unrelenting care of the men during the fort's siege.

Location: Fort Ridgely Historic Site, 72404 County Road 30, Fairfax MN 55332. **GPS:** 44.453113°, -94.734088°.

Hours: Grounds open daily from dawn to dusk.

Phone: (507) 628-5591

Amenities: Fort Ridgely State Park to the east offers cabins and camping, golf, horseback riding, hiking, and biking in a woodland and prairie setting.

Related Sites: There are important sites nearby relating to the Dakota Wars, including the **Birch Coulee Battlefield** (16 miles northwest) and the **Lower Sioux Agency State Historic Site** (13 miles northwest), both near Morton.

Fort Ripley

LITTLE FALLS, MORRISON COUNTY

When the U.S. government moved the Ho-Chunk from northern Iowa to a reservation along the Mississippi River in the Minnesota Territory, it needed a fort to protect them from the nearby warring Dakota and Ojibwe as well as to separate those two tribes. A site was selected deep in the wilderness of the Northwoods on the western bank of the Mississippi, 7 miles south of its confluence with the Crow Wing River.

Construction began in November 1848 on what was originally called Fort Marcy, then Fort Gaines in 1849, and finally Fort Ripley in 1850 after Brig. Gen. Eleazar W. Ripley, a hero of the War of 1812. Its first garrison arrived from Fort Snelling in 1849 under the command of Capt. John B. Todd. The post included several one-and-a-half story buildings, with blockhouses on the northwest and southwest quarters, a palisade wall on the east, and an open parade ground toward the west and the river. With more than fifty-seven thousand acres of heavy woods surrounding the military reservation, this land was much desired by new settlers to the area and meant friction between the military and civilians for years to come.

Friction with the Indians did not happen, however. In fact, after the Ho-Chunk moved near Mankato in 1855, it was so quiet that the army garrison was withdrawn in 1857. The Ojibwe immediately began conflict with settlers, though, and troops quickly returned.

During the Civil War, Fort Ripley's troops were sent to fight against the Confederacy, leaving Minnesota volunteers to staff the fort, and their inexperience opened the door for the Dakota Uprising in 1862 to the south in the Minnesota River valley. Chief Hole-in-the-Day of the Ojibwe planned a simultaneous war around the fort, but settlers moved into Fort Ripley which discouraged any attacks. The fort became the headquarters and supply depot for the campaigns that eventually forced the Dakota west and out of Minnesota.

22. View of Fort Ripley in 1862, looking west across the Mississippi River. Courtesy Minnesota Historical Society.

Troops returned after the Civil War ended and peace ensued. The government moved the Ojibwe to a new reservation much further north, ending the post's importance. An overheated chimney exploded in 1877 and destroyed the laundry, commissary, and officers' quarters. Rather than rebuild, the War Department closed the fort in 1878.

Part of the fort's military reservation in time became Camp Ripley, the heavily wooded training grounds of the Minnesota National Guard. Not only do state and U.S. troops currently train at Camp Ripley, but units from Canada, Great Britain, Norway, and the Netherlands train there as well. The original Fort Ripley grounds are closed to the public but there is little to see—the fort's buildings are gone, as only the stone ruins of the old powder magazine remain. Some building sites are marked, and a flagstaff marks the parade ground, but the site is restricted to military personnel.

However, visitors can see the site from the east side of the Mississippi River. The small village of Fort Ripley is north of the military camp's entrance on Highway 371, and on the north end of the village is a turnoff to an attractive polished black granite marker on which is the history of Fort Ripley. You can drive or walk the short distance south of the marker to the turnaround and view the site of old Fort Ripley. GPS: Marker: 46.179568°, -94.364715°.

Open to civilians (with state-issued driver's license or ID) on the Camp Ripley grounds is the **Minnesota Military Museum,** in a building inspired by those at old Fort Ripley. Besides exhibits sharing the military history of the state, there is also a substantial exhibit on Forts on the Frontier, covering the Dakota War with artifacts and images from the forts and the conflict. A wonderful outdoor display includes military vehicles from World War I through the present.

Location: Minnesota Military Museum, Camp Ripley, 15000 Highway 115, Little Falls MN 56345. **GPS:** 46.075251°, -94.347923°.

Hours: Open daily May through September, 10:00 a.m. to 5:00 p.m.; open Thursday through Saturday, October through April, 10:00 a.m. to 4:00 p.m.

Admission: Fee charged

Amenities: Museum, gift shop, restrooms, and picnic tables.

Phone: (320) 616-6050

Website: mnmilitarymuseum.org

Fort Snelling

ST. PAUL, HENNEPIN COUNTY

Seeking to disrupt and take over the lucrative fur trade enjoyed by the British on the northwest American frontier, in 1819 the United States started to build forts along major waterways to promote trade between native tribes and American traders. The new posts included Fort Howard near Lake Michigan, Fort Atkinson on the Missouri River (see page 90), Forts Armstrong (page 4) and Crawford (page 10) on the Mississippi River, and Fort Snelling at the confluence of the Mississippi and the Minnesota.

Col. Josiah Snelling led the troops who built the fortress on the rocky crag overlooking the rivers, completing the post in 1825. Unlike many other forts of the region and era, they built Fort Snelling with stone to ensure its permanence. It soon won the hearts of the indigenous tribes through gifts, fair trade, and a little intimidation. Its troops enforced treaties and laws, kept the whites out of Indian lands, apprehended outlaws, and because the rivers were open only to U.S. citizens, fur traders made their deals at Fort Snelling rather than north in Canada.

After the Minnesota Territory was opened to white settlement in 1851, Fort Snelling became a supply post and recruitment and training center during

23. Historic Fort Snelling on its rocky cliff above the Mississippi and Minnesota River confluence.

24. Fort Snelling, as painted by Col. Seth Eastman when he was commander of the post in the 1840s. Courtesy Wikimedia Commons.

the Civil War and the Dakota Uprising. Col. Henry Sibley led four hastily armed companies out of the fort against the Dakota during the 1862 uprising, and the river bottoms below the fort were a concentration camp for more than 1,600 Dakota (mostly women, children, and elderly) after the uprising. In the punitive expeditions into the Dakota Territory against the Indians in spring 1863 through late summer 1864, Fort Snelling continued as a supply, stock, and training center. The fort was the location of the final incident of the uprising after federal officials abducted Dakota leaders Shakopee (Little Six) and Medicine Bottle in Canada in late 1864. The government imprisoned, tried, convicted, and hanged the two outside of the fort in 1865.

Fort Snelling became headquarters for the Department of Dakota in the Plains Indian Wars, commanding more than a dozen forts from the Mississippi River to the Rockies. It supplied troops for the campaigns of the 1880s through their conclusion and for the Spanish-American War in 1898. Between the wars, much of the deteriorating stone portions of the fort were demolished to make room for new barracks, officers' quarters, and storehouses.

The fort was a plush assignment leading up to and after World War I, with parades, band concerts, athletic contests, and polo matches as activities, and amenities such as a golf course, tennis courts, a swimming pool, and a hunting club. That ended in 1941 with the attack on Pearl Harbor; during World War II, the fort processed and trained hundreds of thousands of soldiers. It also hosted a unique Japanese language and intelligence school that graduated more than six thousand Japanese Americans for service in Washington DC and the Pacific Ocean.

Following the war, the U.S. Army no longer needed Fort Snelling and the Veterans Administration took over its grounds for use as a hospital. Already substantially changed from its founding, the fort site seemed destined for destruction in the 1950s when plans for a freeway were introduced that would cut through the fort. Such a fate for one of Minnesota's first landmarks was too grim for many members of the public. They succeeded in diverting the freeway project, saving the ruins, and gaining Fort Snelling's designation in 1960 as the state's first National Historic Landmark. Public and private efforts continued to rebuild the fort, which were completed in 1983.

Historic Fort Snelling is Minnesota's most visited historic attraction, not only for its location between the Twin Cities, but because the Minnesota Historical Society runs a truly remarkable restoration and interpretive program at the post. In 2022, the society completed a two-year revitalization

25. Reenactors drilling on the Fort Snelling parade ground.

project, which includes the new Plank Museum and Visitor Center in the former 1904 U.S. Army Cavalry barracks and va clinic building. From the visitor center is a short walk over the busy and hidden Minnesota Highway 5 to the historic fort, and once you pass the sentries posted at the gatehouse you're immediately immersed in the post's early days.

If visiting in the summer, living history surrounds you with drills and musket fire, laundresses and blacksmiths, carpenters and cooks, and fur traders and artists; even Colonel Snelling and his wife are there to tell you about the difficulty and the rewards of frontier fort life. (Living history programs are also offered on weekends in the spring and fall.)

Fifteen structures at Fort Snelling are rebuilt or restored to their original condition and purpose. The most photographed is the Round Tower, which—once you climb to its top—also provides the best view of the fort. Directly across the grounds from the tower is the Commanding Officer's House, beautifully detailed and finished, housing the colonel and his wife. Behind the quarters is the half-moon battery that overlooks the confluence of the Mississippi (to your left) and the Minnesota (to your right), giving a commanding view, although tall trees block the view of the rivers but provide substantial shade for the hiking and biking trails at Fort Snelling State Park.

26. General Snelling House.

The Officers' Quarters, the Round Tower, and Commanding Officer's House are the three original buildings within the Old Fort. Most of the other buildings—including the sutler's store, stone barracks, and the hospital—also have living history interpreters to satisfy your curiosity. Site staff offer tours, but the fort's map can adequately guide you through. Expect to spend a minimum of two hours at the fort, although you could easily spend half a day.

Location: Historic Fort Snelling, 200 Tower Avenue, St. Paul MN 55111. The fort is at the junction of Minnesota Highways 5 and 55, 1 mile east of the Twin Cities International Airport. To get there can be a little tricky in the "spaghetti soup" of highways but watch for signs directing you to "Historic Fort Snelling." *Do not* follow the signs for Fort Snelling State Park, as they won't take you to the fort. **GPS**: 44.892775°, -93.181141°.

Hours: Open daily in summer, Wednesday through Sunday, 10:00 a.m. to 4:00 p.m.; open in off-season, Thursday through Saturday, 10:00 a.m. to 4:00 p.m. Open Memorial Day weekend and Independence Day; closed Thanksgiving, Christmas, New Year's Eve, and New Year's Day.

Admission: Entrance and parking fees

Amenities: Visitor center, gift shop, museum, guided tours, historic buildings, walking trails, refreshments, and restrooms.

Phone: (612) 726-1171

Email: ftsnelling@mnhs.org

Website: mnhs.org/fortsnelling

Glencoe Fort

GLENCOE, MCLEOD COUNTY

Local citizens built Glencoe Fort in August 1862 on the highest point in their community, situated between Fort Snelling and Fort Ridgely. It was the first fort built for protection in the Dakota Uprising and picked up the nickname "Fort Skedaddle," likely due to the pace of settlers in getting there when feeling threatened. A boulder marker for the fort and an information panel are at the site of the Glencoe water tower, across the street from the actual fort site.

Location: 15th Street East and Baxter Avenue North, Glencoe MN. **GPS:** 44.774120°, -94.159655°.

Hutchinson Stockade

HUTCHINSON, MCLEOD COUNTY

The citizens of Hutchinson built a stockade with eight-foot walls at the center of town soon after the Dakota outbreak in August 1862. More than four hundred people were within its walls when Chief Little Crow of the Mdewakanton Dakota and his men attacked it on September 4, one of the few fort defenses assaulted during the uprising. The structure withstood the attack, so the Dakota instead burned structures surrounding it while attacking white civilians nearby. In 1905 a local resident, using his Belgian and Percheron stallions, hauled a massive boulder to the site—now occupied by the town library—and affixed a plaque to commemorate the stockade.

Location: Northwest corner of the Hutchinson Public Library, 50 Hassan Street SE, Hutchinson MN 55350. **GPS:** 44.892109°, -94.368075°.

27. An 1862 photograph of Little Crow, taken by a Hutchinson photographer. Courtesy National Portrait Gallery, Smithsonian Institution.

Maine Prairie Corners Fort

MAINE PRAIRIE TOWNSHIP, STEARNS COUNTY

Settlers from Maine established the village of Maine Prairie Corners near Carnelian Lake in 1856 and joined other communities in building a fort during the 1862 Dakota Uprising. This was a two-story tamarack log structure, reported by the settlers in the *St. Paul Weekly Pioneer and Democrat* as able to withstand a two-month siege of five hundred Indians, but they never had a chance to test their claim. Most of the town moved to nearby Kimball after the railroad routed tracks there in 1886, but Maine Prairie Township still exists; across from its offices on Minnesota Highway 15 is a granite marker placed in 1949 with a brief history and mention of its fort.

Location: 4.75 miles north of Kimball on Minnesota Highway 15, just south of its junction with County Road 8. **GPS:** 45.380550°, -94.267350°.

New Ulm Defenses

NEW ULM, BROWN COUNTY

New Ulm was ripe for attack by the Dakota after the start of the 1862 uprising. It was the largest settlement near their reservation, offering the most supplies and goods to deal with their famine. The tiered land on which New Ulm was built was difficult for townspeople to defend, and many of its young men left to fight in the Civil War and took most of the town's firearms and ammunition with them.

The citizens of New Ulm turned out on the morning of August 18 to give their well-wishes to recruits leaving to fight in the war. The Dakota ambushed those men at nearby Milford, however, and surviving recruits rushed back to New Ulm just as farm families were coming into town with word of the attacks. Although thrown into panic, citizens quickly erected barricades between the stronger brick buildings of New Ulm and created a three-block fortress for their protection. They appealed to surrounding towns for help, and one of those responding was Charles Eugene Flandrau. Already one of the best-known citizens of Minnesota, Flandrau helped settle new German immigrants, served as an Indian agent, was a member of the Minnesota constitutional convention, and served as a justice of the Minnesota Supreme Court before rushing to New Ulm's defense.

Refugees swarmed into New Ulm and built up the barricade walls as attacks continued in the countryside. The first assault on the town began on the afternoon of August 19 when the Dakota fired from the bluff onto the makeshift fort below, but an evening thunderstorm, a lack of leadership, and a coordinated defense helped drive them off. Flandrau and other volunteers arrived in New Ulm that night, immediately increasing the size and strength of the barricades. The town elected Flandrau as commander of the defense,

28. Charles Eugene Flandrau. Courtesy Library of Congress.

giving him the rank of colonel. More volunteers arrived in the following days, boosting the number to around three hundred citizen-soldiers there to protect more than 1,700 civilians.

On the morning of August 23, about 650 warriors led by Dakota chiefs Mankato, Wabasha, and Big Eagle attacked New Ulm from the west. Flandrau counterattacked, leading around forty men over the wall, yelling and cheering, to disrupt the Dakota and cause them to turn and retreat. The battle turned and by night it was over. Flandrau ordered the buildings outside the boundary of the fort burned to remove cover for the Dakota.

29. New Ulm artist Anton Gag painted this flour barrelhead in 1902 with a scene of the battle for the town and its defenses. It is now displayed at the Brown County History Museum. Courtesy Brown County Historical Society.

The Indians returned the next morning for a brief show of force but soon left. The siege left New Ulm depleted of ammunition, food, and supplies, as well as suffering under poor sanitation, so the people evacuated for Mankato on August 25. The Dakota killed thirty-four and wounded sixty in the two attacks; the tribe's casualties were unknown.

The largest American town ever attacked by native peoples, New Ulm rebuilt as one of Minnesota's most beautiful and historic communities. The 1862 fortress built for its defense soon disappeared, but signs of it and of the Dakota Uprising are found in buildings, monuments, markers, and plaques while walking the downtown streets.

The first stop on any self-guided tour should be the **Brown County History Museum** in New Ulm. Built in 1909 to serve as the town's post office, the distinctive Renaissance Revival "gingerbread" design reflects the town's German heritage; today it's the center attraction of New Ulm's historic past. The museum's first two floors include the general history of the county and special exhibits, but those with a special interest in the Indian Wars and Brown County's particular role should visit the third floor. Updated in 2022 for the 160th anniversary of the U.S.-Dakota War, the museum's exhibit summarizes the causes, events, and lasting effects of the conflict.

Along with narratives exploring how differences led to the war, the museum offers some amazing artifacts such as a batter cannon used in the New Ulm defense, a wagon used to rescue settlers from the nearby settlement of Leavenworth, firearms, and even Chief Little Crow's flute. Spend at least an hour with the museum before taking the downtown walk.

Location: Brown County History Museum, 2 North Broadway, New Ulm MN 56073. **GPS:** 44.312867°, -94.460288°.

Hours: Tuesday through Friday, 10:00 a.m. to 4:00 p.m.

Admission: Fee charged

Phone: (507) 233-2616

Email: director@browncountyhistorymn.org

The museum has a brochure and guides available on the New Ulm defenses, as well as interpretive signage on the front lawn. Buildings existing during the attacks and markers in the area include:

The **Kiesling House** (220 North Minnesota Street), near the northeast corner of the defenses, is one of three buildings still standing since the war. Then

30. The 1861 Kiesling House, one of three downtown buildings in New Ulm to survive the Dakota's attack.

the home of blacksmith and farrier Frederick W. Kiesling, the 1861 frame home was to be torched if the Dakota broke through. Now managed by the Brown County Historical Society. Hours: Open Memorial Day through Labor Day, Friday and Saturday, noon to 4:00 p.m. Admission fee charged. Phone: (507) 233-2621

The nearby **Grand Hotel** (212 North Minnesota Street) was the 1862 site of the Union Hotel, used as a hospital during the attacks. One of the attending physicians was the father of William and Charles Mayo, founders of the Mayo Clinic. A large plaque at the front door of the hotel tells the story.

The **Erd Building** (108 North Minnesota Street) was a refuge for women and children during the attacks; defenders kept a keg of gunpowder in the middle of their basement hiding place, which was to be ignited if the Dakota breached the walls.

The **Dacotah House** (105 North Minnesota Street) served as a hospital, refuge center, and military headquarters in the battles. A modern building now stands at the site with a bronze plaque near its doorway.

A marker to **Flandrau's Charge,** which changed the tide of the battle, is on South Minnesota Street, south of 1st South Street on the east side of the road.

Norway Lake Military Post

NEW LONDON, KANDIYOHI COUNTY

Another post built in 1865 to restore settler confidence in returning to the Minnesota frontier was on the west bank of Norway Lake. A company of the 2nd Minnesota Volunteer Cavalry manned the post, which featured dummy cannons at the corners of the 100-by-250-foot fort to frighten off attackers. The regiment abandoned the post in 1866.

Location: An information kiosk about the fort is off the parking lot of the First Lutheran Church of Norway Lake, 9 miles west of New London, at 6338 County Road 40 NW, New London MN 56273. To reach the fort site, continue west for 1 mile on County Road 40 to County Highway 1 NW; turn right (north) for 2 miles and look for a small sign dedicated to the post at the intersection of County Road 1 NW and 210th Avenue NW. **GPS:** Information Kiosk: 45.296548°, -95.130067°; Fort Site: 45.325847°, -95.152455°.

Ole Jorgenson's Stockade ★

Militia built a small stockade on the farm of Norwegian immigrant Ole Jorgenson for the protection of his family and other settlers during the 1862 uprising. It was never attacked, although one of the soldiers—Ole Boxrud—was killed. The eighteen-year-old Boxrud was on guard duty at the Jorgenson house when barking dogs warned of Dakota nearby; rather than stay in the house, he ran to warn his fellow soldiers in the stockade and was killed before reaching it. An historical marker at the Jorgenson homestead recounts the incident.

Location: The marker is east of the intersection of 335th Street (County Road 16) and 780th Avenue (County Road 118), about 7 miles northeast of St. James. **GPS:** 44.000400°, -94.497383°.

Pike's Fort ☆

The first U.S. military fort built on the Northern Plains was a small stockade built in the fall of 1805 during the expedition of Lt. Zebulon M. Pike on the west bank of the Mississippi River, near the mouth of the Swan River. The thirty-six-foot square structure, with blockhouses at two corners, was built to hold men and equipment over the winter while Pike continued up the Mississippi by sled. He returned from his explorations in April, with the expedition party traveling downriver by boat.

Local historians found the site of Pike's stockade south of Little Falls in 1880. They marked it with an inscribed boulder reading "Pike's Fort Built 1805," and in 1919 the local DAR chapter improved upon that with a pyramidal monument using rocks from the fort's fireplace.

Location: The monument is today on private property but is available to view by contacting the nearby Charles A. Weyerhaeuser Memorial Museum, located at 2151 South Lindbergh Drive, Little Falls, MN 56345, (320) 632-4007, or by emailing staff@morrisoncountyhistory.org. There is also a small metal sign commemorating Pike's Wintering Quarters on the Swan River bridge, approximately 3.5 miles south of Little Falls on South Lindbergh Drive. **GPS:** Metal Sign: 45.918721°, -94.389063°.

Pomme de Terre Stockade ☆

ASHBY, GRANT COUNTY

Company D of the 8th Minnesota in 1863 built Pomme de Terre Stockade on a hilltop close to an existing trail between Pembina at the Canadian border and Fort Snelling. The Dakota never attacked but did kill two soldiers looking for goose eggs to supplement their rations; Cpl. Zenas Blackman and Pvt. H. Adam Hare were buried near the fort. The local American Legion post in 1933 placed a small monument at the site to commemorate them. (Of note to the reader, the French-to-English translation for "pomme de terre" is typically "potato," but the historical reference is to the prairie turnip, a popular staple for the Dakota. The fort took its name from the nearby river and lake of the same name).

Location: This monument is on a private farm, 4.75 miles southwest of Ashby on County Road 4; obtain permission before attempting to visit. The **Grant County Museum**, located at 115 2nd Street NE, Elbow Lake MN 56531, (218) 685-4864, has a diorama of the fort and artifacts from the site.

Redwood Stockade

REDWOOD FALLS, REDWOOD COUNTY

Samuel McPhail—an early Minnesota pioneer and a commander during the Dakota Uprising—built a stockade at Redwood Falls in 1863 for the protection of his cabin, the post office, and other buildings. In 1962 during the centennial of the uprising the Redwood County Centennial Committee installed a granite marker at the county courthouse to commemorate the fort.

Location: Redwood County Courthouse, 250 South Jefferson Street, Redwood Falls MN 56283. **GPS:** 44.539711°, -95.116513°.

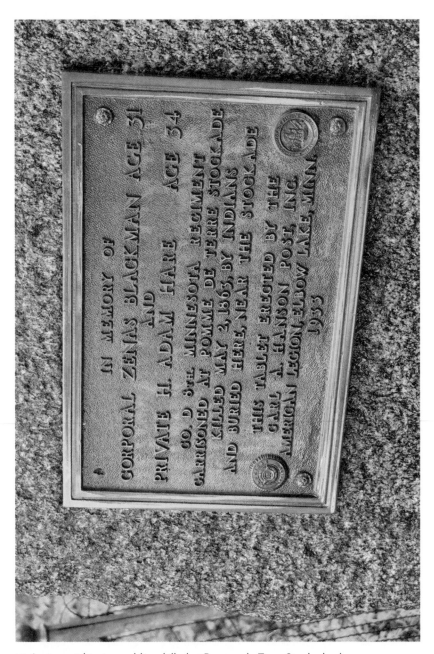

31. A memorial to two soldiers killed at Pomme de Terre Stockade also serves as a marker to the fort.

32. Memorial Park monument to the St. Joseph Blockhouse.

St. Joseph Blockhouse   ★

ST. JOSEPH, STEARNS COUNTY

Citizens of St. Joseph built three pentagonal blockhouses—each with fifty-foot-long sides and one-foot-thick walls of green timber—during the Dakota Uprising to discourage attacks along the essential Red River Trail. The Work Projects Administration built a monument-plaza to one of the forts in 1941 on the grounds of Memorial Park in St. Joseph.

   Location: Southwest corner of Old U.S. Highway 52 (West Birch Street) and 2nd Avenue NW, St. Joseph MN. **GPS:** 45.566333°, -94.322800°.

Sauk Centre Stockade   ★

SAUK CENTRE, STEARNS COUNTY

The people of Sauk Centre built a stockade for their defense in August 1862, which soldiers expanded to a three-acre fort the following year. One of the largest civilian posts on the Minnesota frontier, the Sauk Centre fort maintained vital communications between St. Cloud and Fort Abercrombie in the Dakota Territory until its abandonment in 1865. Townspeople dedicated a granite boulder and plaque in 1916 to commemorate the fort with former occupants attending, including two of the children born in the stockade.

   Location: Northeast corner of Birch Street South and Seventh Street South. **GPS:** 45.732146°, -94.948639°.

Legend:
- ■ Staffed Fort Site
- ☐ Unstaffed Site
- ⬡ No Public Access

Fort Peck

Fort Assiniboine

OLD FORT BENTON

Camp Cooke

Fort Maginnis

Powder River Depot

MILES CITY

FORT KEOGH

Fort Pease

Fort Custer

Fort C.F. Smith

GREAT FALLS

Fort Logan

BILLINGS

Fort Shaw

Fort Ellis

BOZEMAN

HELENA

MISSOULA

FORT MISSOULA

Fort Fizzle

BUTTE

4. Forts of Montana

FORTS OF MONTANA

Montana represented the final frontier of western expansion into the Northern Plains by Euro-American arrivals, who naturally had their chapters of commerce and conflict with the native peoples living there, including the Lakota Sioux, Cheyenne, Blackfeet, and Nez Perce.

Fort Benton served as a crucial trading post and supply center for the early settlers and fur traders of the region, only assuming a military role toward the end of its activity. Fort Shaw was built to protect the road between Fort Benton and Idaho goldfields and Fort Custer went up to prevent more conflicts with the Lakota and Cheyenne after the Battle of the Little Bighorn. Posts like Fort Missoula and Fort Keogh were constructed to protect new settlers and maintain order.

The forts of Montana are well represented in tourism sites, existing and preserved buildings, and historical markers. Fort Benton is a popular attraction as a National Historic Landmark, with its reconstructed structures and the oldest building in the state. Fort Missoula and its buildings likewise share historical interpretation and events; Fort Shaw and Fort Assiniboine are partially preserved, offering some interpretation; Fort Keogh is almost entirely gone, save for a preserved building and a great interpretive display at a nearby museum.

Camp Cooke ★

The War Department chose the site of Camp Cooke in July 1866 near the confluence of the Judith River with the Missouri River. This was Montana's first military post, built to protect river traffic to and from the Montana goldfields, but the only thing it protected was itself. There were no people or property within miles, and the only attacks it received in its first year were from newspapers criticizing its location. Indians attacked the fort in May 1868, but the camp held them off, even with only five officers and slightly more than a hundred men. The U.S. Army abandoned the post by 1870 with most of its supplies going to Fort Benton. Today two small signs, separated by the Missouri River at the Judith Landing site, commemorate Camp Cooke.

Location: The signs are about 23 miles northwest of Winifred on the unpaved PN Bridge Road (Montana Highway 236). The first is at the intersection 1 mile south of the Missouri River bridge—look for the much larger "Judith Landing" historical marker. The second is a quarter-mile north of the bridge on Highway 236 in Chouteau County. **GPS**: First Marker: -47.726026°, -109.634692°. Second Marker: 47.741661°, -109.625272°.

Fort Assiniboine

Fort Assiniboine, named for a nearby tribe along the Montana-Canada border, was already obsolete when it opened in 1879. The fort had a million-dollar price tag and more than one hundred buildings, most of them made of brick, but its immense size belied its small tasks of patrolling the border and keeping First Nations people of Canada away from American reservations. The army maintained and expanded the fort but found it surplus property by 1900. The federal government formally abandoned Fort Assiniboine in 1911.

The fort site is now Montana State University's Northern Agricultural Research Center. A few of the fort's original brick buildings survive and are marked, including the Company Officers' Quarters (built in 1880), the library (1889), and the post exchange (1879). A large marker commemorates

33. The turreted company officers' quarters is one several remaining structures of Fort Assiniboine.

the fort, placed by the local chapter of the DAR. The Fort Assiniboine Preservation Association occasionally offers tours of the site; check its website at fortassinniboine.org for information.

Location: MSU Northern Agricultural Research Center, 3710 Assiniboine Road, Havre MN 59501. The site is approximately 7 miles southwest of Havre, or a half-mile south of the junction of U.S. Highway 87 and 82nd Avenue West. A state highway marker to the fort is to the east of the junction, on U.S. Highway 87. **GPS**: Site Marker: 48.498567°, -109.796523°; U.S. Highway 87 Marker: 48.507490°, -109.798651°.

Fort Benton

Fort Benton (named for U.S. Senator and westward-expansionist Thomas Hart Benton of Missouri) began life as an adobe fur trade post in 1846, but truly came into its own after the mining of Montana gold began in 1862. The gold rush coincided with the advent of steamboats up the Missouri River, and traffic boomed to Fort Benton—more than 2,700 river miles from the Gulf of Mexico—as the world's innermost port. Millions of tons of goods and supplies arrived at Fort Benton for the mines and the settlements surrounding them, with gold, furs, and buffalo robes shipped downstream for points east.

Mining declined in the Montana Territory by the late 1860s, however, and the War Department wanted to use Fort Benton as a forwarding point for supplies and mail to other posts. It never stationed more than a company of men at the fort from 1869 to 1881, and at one point only a solitary officer and five enlisted men ran the fort, though they rented houses in town due to the fort's dilapidated condition. The town of Fort Benton lost more than half its population after the gold boom and was more than happy to rent space to the army until abandoning the fort in 1881.

Steamboats disappeared with the arrival of the railroad, but Fort Benton remained as one Montana's most historic towns. In fact, the "birthplace of Montana" has an amazing number of museums for a town of only around 1,400. Operated by the River and Plains Society as part of their Fort Benton Museums and Heritage Complex, the first stop is **Old Fort Benton** at the north end of town on the Missouri River shoreline. This is the fort's original site, and it holds an original blockhouse—the oldest building in the state. Old Fort Benton puts its emphasis on the fur trade history; the steamboat, gold rush, and Indian Wars years are part of the adjacent Museum of the Upper Missouri, with displays on the history and legends of the river country. The Starr Gallery of Western Art in the fort's Bourgeois House features sculptures and rare art, including prints from Swiss painter Karl Bodmer's travels through the area with Prince Maximilian of Sweden. Of note to the visitor: the River and Plains Society is reconstructing the fort to make it as historically accurate as possible following archaeological excavations and extensive research, so you may encounter some construction.

34. Fort Benton began as a fur-trading post on the Missouri River, memorialized at the Old Fort Park (*foreground*).

35. An original blockhouse from Fort Benton (*at right*) stands as the oldest building in Montana.

Location: Old Fort Benton, Old Fort Park, Fort Benton MT 59442. GPS: 47.821222°, -110.663796°.

Hours: Open daily in tourism season; closed October through Memorial Day.

Admission: Fee charged

Phone: (406) 622-5316

Website: fortbentonmuseums.com

Admission to the Old Fort Benton museum also gives the traveler access to another museum complex just a few blocks away. The **Museum of the Northern Great Plains**, with the story of the settlement of the area over the past century, also includes Homesteader Village, showcasing a rural community of the 1900s; the Hornaday Smithsonian Buffalo, its stuffed bison bull the model for U.S. coin, currency, and postage stamps; and the Strand Western Art Gallery, featuring nineteenth century western art.

Location: Museum of the Northern Great Plains, 1205 20th Street, Fort Benton MT 59442. GPS: 47.824433°, -110.666920°.

Hours: Open daily in tourism season; closed October through Memorial Day.

The Upper Missouri River Breaks National Monument Interpretive Center highlights the natural and cultural history of the area, but those with an interest in the Plains Indian Wars will find here the rifle of Nez Perce leader Chief Joseph; he raised it over his head when he gave his unforgettable speech, "From where the sun now stands, I will fight no more forever."

Location: 701 7th Street, Fort Benton MT 59442. GPS: 47.810227°, -110.673112°.

Admission: Fee charged

Hours: Open Tuesday through Saturday in tourism season; closed October through Memorial Day.

Phone: (406) 622-4000

Fort C. F. Smith

FORT SMITH, BIG HORN COUNTY

Fort C. F. Smith, (named for a Civil War general) on the Bighorn River joined Fort Reno and Fort Phil Kearney in Wyoming in 1866 to secure the Bozeman Trail. The Lakota and Cheyenne subjected the trail and the forts to constant harassment. Mail, food, and supplies barely trickled in on the dangerous trail during its first year, so a supply train of food and soldiers in June 1867, followed by a shipment of new breech-loading Springfield rifles the next month, were timely. On August 1, 1867, Lakota, Cheyenne, and Arapaho attacked a handful of soldiers and hay cutters 2.5 miles northeast of the fort. The men and their new guns held off their attackers at the Hayfield Fight, as the attack came to be known.

Conditions improved at the fort through additional supplies and structure improvements, and it became safe enough to even bring the officers' families. The 1868 treaty with the Lakota required the fort's abandonment by July 28, however, and soon afterward the Lakota destroyed Fort C. F. Smith. All signs of the fort are gone today except for slight rises showing the location of its adobe walls. A local women's club placed a stone marker to the fort in 1933.

Location: The marker is on private land about a half-mile north of the town of Fort Smith; permission should be sought for viewing. GPS: 45.314637°, -107.908686°.

Note: The site of the **Hayfield Fight** is 2.5 miles north of Fort Smith off Highway 313 and open to the public. GPS: 45.335167°, -107.867636°.

36. This marker to Fort Custer formerly stood at the fort site on the bluff in the distance, and now stands at the Big Horn County Historical Museum.

Fort Custer

Built in 1877 on a bluff overlooking the confluence of the Bighorn and Little Bighorn Rivers, the War Department named Fort Custer for Col. George A. Custer, killed the year before at the Battle of the Little Bighorn. The fort's purpose was to control the Lakota of the area, earlier forced by the government to reservations. Fort Custer supplied some troops for the Bannock War of 1878 and for an uprising at the nearby Crow Agency in 1886, but that was the extent of its participation in the Plains Indian Wars. It was abandoned in 1898 with its buildings sold to the public, one of which still stands in Fort Smith as a bed-and-breakfast.

The local DAR chapter commemorated Fort Custer with a large granite marker and plaque at the site in 1930, moved in recent years a mile north and across the river to the **Big Horn County Historical Museum** (1163 3rd Street East, Hardin MT 59034). The museum's regional exhibits include Fort Custer on the Big Horn, featuring the Fort Custer Stagecoach, uniforms, weapons, artifacts, photographs, and a scale model of the fort.

Hours: Open daily Memorial Day to Labor Day, 8:00 a.m. to 6:00 p.m.; open Monday through Friday, Labor Day to Memorial Day, 9:00 a.m. to 5:00 p.m.

Admission: Fee charged

Phone: (406) 665-1671

Website: bighorncountymuseum.org

Note: Little Bighorn Battlefield National Monument is 14 miles to the southeast off I-90.

Fort Ellis

A key fort to the Indian Wars campaigns of Montana, Fort Ellis initially provided protection to settlers to the Gallatin Valley southwest of Bozeman in 1867. In the 1870s, however, companies of the 2nd Cavalry and 7th Infantry were here, participating in the tragic "Marais Massacre" of 1870, and Col. John Gibbon's "Montana Column" was present in the 1876 Little Bighorn campaign and the Nez Perce War of 1877. The railroad came to Bozeman in

1881 and homesteader pressure for the fort's reservation brought Fort Ellis's closure in 1886. The grounds are now home to Montana State University's Agriculture Experimental Station.

Location: There are two markers to Fort Ellis at Bozeman. The first and closest to the site is a 1926 DAR marker southeast of Bozeman at a pull-off on Old Route 191, east of its intersection with Fort Ellis Road and north of the university agricultural station. Another marker to Fort Ellis is found at the Bozeman I-90 rest area on 19th Avenue near the eastbound entrance ramp. **GPS:** DAR Marker: 45.668573°, -110.975248°. Rest Stop Marker: 45.712363°, -111.064168°.

37. The replica entrenchment of Fort Fizzle.

Fort Fizzle

LOLO, MISSOULA COUNTY

Receiving word in July 1877 of "hostile Nez Perce" approaching the Lolo Trail west of Missoula, Capt. Charles Rawn and about thirty-five soldiers were ordered to block their passage. Rawn selected a slight terrace to construct an earth-and-log breastwork, aided in their construction and defense by more than two hundred citizen volunteers. Four miles west of the ad-hoc fortress, however, troops met the Nez Perce and demanded they give up their weapons and horses; the tribe refused and promised to pass peacefully. The volunteers took them at their word and abandoned the breastworks to guard their homes, and the Nez Perce took a different route to bypass the soldiers. The defense was a successful failure and thus "Fort Fizzle" was named.

A replica of the entrenchment with interpretive panels is at a wayside park in Lolo National Forest, and restrooms are available.

Location: 4 miles west of Lolo on U.S. Highway 12. **GPS:** 46.7463°, -114.172°.

Fort Keogh ★★★

MILES CITY, CUSTER COUNTY

Col. Nelson A. Miles established a base camp in 1877 near the confluence of the Tongue and Yellowstone Rivers for the Lakota campaign. Also known as the New Post on the Yellowstone and Tongue River Barracks, its official name became Fort Keogh in 1878 in honor of Capt. Myles W. Keogh, killed at the Little Bighorn battle. The post's location in southeast Montana enabled its forces to strike fast and hard against the warring Lakota, constantly harassing them to keep moving and leave valuable horses and supplies behind. Colonel Miles developed a reputation as one of the most successful Indian fighters during the late 1870s and early 1880s, defeating Sitting Bull, Crazy Horse, Lame Deer, and Chief Joseph in separate engagements.

Fort Keogh was the largest fort in the territory, encompassing a fifty-five-thousand-acre reservation and hosting around 1,500 men. It served as an infantry and cavalry post until 1908, when it became an army remount station. In 1924 the post became a livestock experiment station with its jurisdiction transferred to the U.S. Department of Agriculture.

The USDA systematically destroyed nearly sixty buildings of old Fort Keogh, and as a result there's not much historically to see at the site. A modern metal placard stands before the headquarters building at the experiment station with a brief history of the fort and the **Fort Keogh Historic District**. The only building remaining from the Indian Wars days at the site is the 1883 brick water wagon shed on the east end of the building complex.

Location: Fort Keogh Livestock and Range Research Laboratory, 243 Fort Keogh Road, Miles City MT 59301 (north of I-94, exit 135). **GPS:** 46.381655°, -105.884348°.

38. An 1883 water wagon shed is the only Indian Wars—era building remaining at Fort Keogh.

A restored original officer's quarters building survives today at the nearby **Range Riders Museum,** one of the best museums of the Old West. Eleven buildings make up the museum complex, including the officer's quarters with an inventory including the fossilized bones of mammoths, the stunning four-hundred-piece Bert Clark Gun Collection, Indian artifacts, Charles Russell artwork, hand tools, quilts, saddles, an Old-West street scene, and much more.

For the fort fanatic, the museum includes a room-sized diorama of Fort Keogh. Photographs taken by famed frontier photographer Christian Barthelmess (the great-grandfather of the museum's current curator, Bunny Miller) highlight the events and people of the fort's history. The collection includes weapons and other items used at the fort, with even Nelson Miles's dress uniform on display. One of the more fascinating inclusions is a handwritten letter from Elizabeth Custer to Colonel Miles, presenting him with one-inch squares of three items from her husband's dramatic history: pieces of the surrender table and truce flag at the battle of Appomattox and a piece of Custer's scarlet neckerchief worn into battle. Expect to spend several hours at the Range Riders Museum, most of them with your jaw dropped to your belt buckle—this is not a place you can rush through.

Location: Range Riders Museum, 435 L. P. Anderson Road, Miles City MT 59301 (west end of Main Street). **GPS:** 46.402848°, -105.863127°.

39. A restored and modified Fort Keogh officer's quarters survives at the nearby Range Riders Museum in Miles City.

Hours: Open from April 15 through October 15, 8:00 a.m. to 5:00 p.m.; closed Tuesdays.

Admission: Fee charged

Phone: (406) 232-6146

Website: rangeridersmuseum.com

Fort Logan

WHITE SULFUR SPRINGS, MEAGER COUNTY

Beginning in 1869 as Camp Baker, a sub-post of Fort Ellis, this Smith River valley post protected Montana gold camps and Missouri River trade and provided troops to other forts. But this was a desolate post—the nearest mining towns were at least 13 miles away and abandoned during the winter. Camp

40. Built in 1869, the Fort Logan blockhouse still stands on the fort's original grounds, although not on its original site.

Baker took the name Fort Logan in 1878 to honor Capt. William Logan, killed in the 1877 Battle of the Big Hole. The "fort" designation indicated permanence, but two years later department headquarters ordered the post vacated.

Fort Logan's grounds became a ranch after its abandonment. Its unique blockhouse survives at the site, although it was moved a short distance in 1962 when Montana Highway 360 was paved. In the town of White Sulfur Springs, 17 miles away, an historical marker and small blockhouse replica commemorate the fort at the town park.

Location: The park is at U.S. Highway 89 and Chilton Street in White Sulfur Springs. **GPS:** 46.546857°, -110.906102°. The fort and ranch site is 17 miles northwest of town on Montana Highway 360. **GPS:** 46.678393°, -111.173702°.

Fort Maginnis ★

LEWISTOWN, FERGUS COUNTY

Built in 1881, Fort Maginnis arrived late to the Plains and was almost unnecessary. Wealthy cattlemen wanted the army there to protect their herds from native rustlers; they also wanted the generous profits from cattle sales to the fort. Even with that convenient arrangement, the fort and cattlemen butted heads immediately over the hay fields claimed by the army. The cattlemen also hated the military policy of sending the native rustlers and stolen livestock to the officially neutral Indian agency—the cattle thief typically escaped justice and the cattlemen had to travel sometimes hundreds of miles to get their livestock back.

Fort Maginnis closed in 1890 and the government sold off its buildings and property. Former railroad surveyor Abraham Hogeland bought two of the officers' quarters in 1895, dismantled them, and moved them to Lewistown for rebuilding. The Hogeland House still stands at 620 West Montana Street (**GPS:** 47.065233°, -109.433274°) with a historical marker in its front yard.

Location: Only vague foundations exist at the Fort Maginnis site, but it is open to the public. From Lewistown, take U.S. Highway 87 east for 13 miles to the unpaved Gilt Edge Road; go north for more than 5.5 miles to a left curve and then take the right fork on Black Butte Road. Go north for 5 more miles until reaching Fort Maginnis Road; drive another 1.5 miles and take the left fork for less than a mile, watching for the ford across the (hopefully dry) Fords Creek. Continuing on the trail, you'll come to a fork with a sign indicating the fort site (**GPS**: 47.184865°, -109.136817°) is to the left and the post cemetery (**GPS**: 47.187644°, -109.147205°) to the right. Foundations and a few tombstones indicate the locations of both.

If you or the weather are not up to this off-the-pavement trek, a historical marker for Fort Maginnis is on U.S. Highway 87, about 2 miles east of Gilt Edge Road turn. **GPS**: 47.062362°, -109.114399°.

41. Only traces of Fort Maginnis' structures remain under the shadows of the Judith Mountains.

Fort Missoula

MISSOULA, MISSOULA COUNTY

Settler fears in Missoula brought the U.S. Army's 7th Infantry and Capt. Charles Rawn to construct the Post at Missoula 4 miles southwest of the town in 1876, renamed Fort Missoula the following year. Its troops served in the Nez Perce War and the Battle of the Big Hole against Chief Joseph. After the Plains Indian Wars in Montana, the fort hosted the 25th Infantry, a "Buffalo Soldier" regiment; those Black American soldiers participated in the 25th Infantry Bicycle Corps, testing riding bicycles across the Plains as a replacement to horses (they didn't).

Troops garrisoned the post through 1898 and then intermittently until the World War I when it was used as an army mechanics school. During World War II, the fort was turned into a prison camp for Italian POWs and housed Japanese Americans who were treated as "enemy aliens" after the attack on Pearl Harbor. The army decommissioned Fort Missoula after the war, and many of the buildings were sold, dismantled, and moved from the site.

Today, most of the former Fort Missoula is part of non-military agencies such as the U.S. Forest Service, Bureau of Land Management, and Missoula County. The latter hosts the **Historical Museum at Fort Missoula**, within

42. The 1880 carriage house (*left*) with 1878 non-commissioned officers' quarters are the two remaining original Fort Missoula buildings still standing.

the fort's 1911 brick Quartermaster Storehouse, housing exhibit galleries, a museum store, and offices. The grounds of the thirty-two-acre museum complex contain more than twenty historic structures, most collected from the city, the nearby region, and later eras of the fort, but only two from the Indian Wars era: a log noncommissioned officer's quarters built in 1878 and a carriage house built in 1880. Both buildings were previously sold and removed from the fort but returned to the grounds after their original purposes were discovered.

Location: Historical Museum at Fort Missoula, 3400 Captain Rawn Way, Missoula MT 59804. **GPS**: 46.842778°, -114.058056°.

Hours: Memorial Day to Labor Day, Monday through Saturday, 10:00 a.m. to 5:00 p.m., Sunday, noon to 5:00 p.m.; Labor Day to Memorial Day, Tuesday through Sunday, noon to 5:00 p.m., closed Mondays.

Admission: Fee charged

Phone: (406) 728-3476

Website: fortmissoulamuseum.com

Fort Pease ★

HYSHAM, TREASURE COUNTY

Businessmen from Bozeman built Fort Pease in 1875 to boost trade on the Yellowstone River, but its location within Lakota hunting grounds meant its continual harassment. The Lakota killed some of the trappers and had the post under siege until troopers from Fort Ellis escorted the surviving trappers back with them. It was thought the Lakota would then destroy the civilian fort, but Col. John Gibbon found it still standing during the 1876 campaign and occupied it for two weeks before meeting General Terry and Lieutenant Colonel Custer at Rosebud Creek on June 21. After Custer's defeat at the battle of the Little Bighorn four days later, Gibbon's Montana Column and the remnants of Custer's 7th Cavalry regrouped at Fort Pease before its abandonment and subsequent burning by the Lakota.

Location: The fort site is unmarked and on private land, but there is a small marker of Fort Pease's history in nearby Hysham at a small downtown park next to the Treasure County 89'ers Museum, 325 Elliott Avenue, Hysham MT 59038. **GPS**: 46.292813°, -107.232463°.

Fort Peck ★

Built as a trading post in 1867, Fort Peck was a three-hundred-square-foot stockade with twelve-foot walls. Although the army never took possession of it, troops and peace commissioners used it as temporary headquarters during negotiations with regional tribes. The trading post eventually became the Indian agency, a function that ended in 1878. Today the fort site lies under the waters of Fort Peck Lake, created with the completion of the Fort Peck Dam in 1940. A state highway marker gives a brief history of the namesake fort.

Location: The marker is at the intersection of Highway 24 and Missouri Avenue (County Road 117) at a pull-off near mile marker 59. **GPS:** 48.000800°, -106.480150°.

Fort Shaw ★★

Named for Col. Robert G. Shaw, commander of the famed all–African American 54th Massachusetts regiment, Fort Shaw was established in 1867 as a buffer between Montana gold camps and the tribes of the Sun River area. Troops protected the stage and shipping trail between Fort Benton and Helena, were part of the burial detail after Custer's 1876 disaster at the Little Bighorn, and fought in the Battle of the Big Hole the next year.

After the War Department closed Fort Shaw in 1891, the post was an Indian school until its closure in 1910. The government granted the property in 1926 to the local school district; today, the Fort Shaw National Historic Site occupies part of the present town's elementary school, with two officers' buildings from the fort surviving. There is a 1931 historical monument on the school grounds across from the quarters, along with a monument to the Indian school's girls' basketball team, which won the "world championship" at the 1904 St. Louis World's Fair. Less than a mile west of the school is the Fort Shaw Military Cemetery. A state marker on Highway 200 southeast of town includes a brief history of the fort.

43. Now home to the Sun River Valley Historical Society, these 1867 officer's quarters are a partial a reminder of Fort Shaw, once known as the "Queen of Montana Forts."

Location: Fort Shaw National Historic Site is a half-mile northwest of Fort Shaw on North Fort Shaw Road with a right turn onto the school loop. GPS: Officers' Quarters: 47.509097°, -111.820930°; Highway Marker: 47.500218°, -111.818938°.

Powder River Depot   ★

TERRY, PRAIRIE COUNTY

Gen. Alfred Terry established the Powder River Depot at the river's conflu-ence with the Yellowstone on June 7, 1876, to supply that year's campaign, including Custer's 7th Cavalry. It continued in that role for the next six years to organize and supply troops to complete the war against the Lakota. The depot was a tent city with no permanent buildings. The grounds (now under the federal Bureau of Land Management) have changed little since the Indian Wars. A dirt road through the site takes you to the graves of Pvt. William George, who died of wounds from the Battle of the Little Bighorn, and of scout Wesley Brockmeyer, killed in a skirmish at the depot on August 2, 1876.

Location: 7 miles west of Terry. Take I-94 exit 169 and go one half-mile north to State Highway 10; turn right after a third of a mile to find an exhibit about the depot. Continue north along the highway, go underneath the railroad bridge, drive up to the bench overlooking the Yellowstone River, and take the dirt road north for a little over 1 mile to the Brockmeyer grave and another third of a mile to the Private George grave. GPS: 46.752461°, -105.429096°.

Amenities: Camping, canoeing, and kayaking are permitted, but there are no facilities or boat launch.

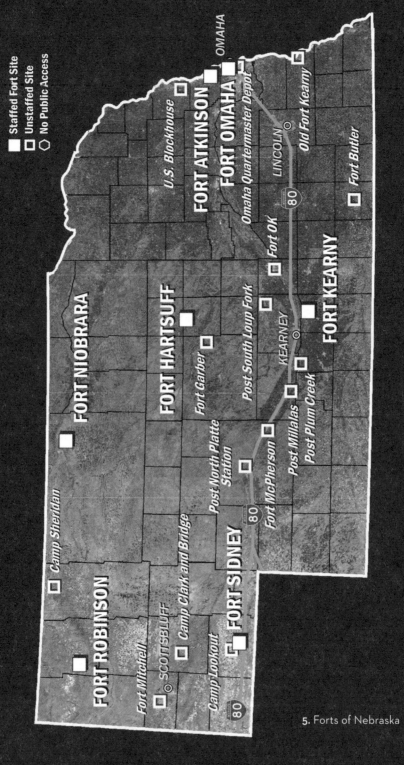

Staffed Fort Site

Unstaffed Site

No Public Access

OMAHA

U.S. Blockhouse

FORT ATKINSON

FORT OMAHA

Omaha Quartermaster Depot

Old Fort Kearny

LINCOLN

Fort Butler

80

Fort OK

FORT NIOBRARA

FORT HARTSUFF

Post South Loup Fork

FORT KEARNY

Fort Garber

KEARNEY

Post North Platte Station

Post Millalas

Post Plum Creek

Camp Sheridan

80

Fort McPherson

FORT ROBINSON

FORT SIDNEY

Camp Clark and Bridge

SCOTTSBLUFF

Camp Lookout

Fort Mitchell

80

5. Forts of Nebraska

FORTS OF NEBRASKA

Located at the confluence of the north-to-south waterway of the Missouri River and the east-to-west route of the Platte River valley, Nebraska naturally became home to a diversity of tribes, including the Oto, Omaha, Ponca, Pawnee, Cheyenne, and Lakota. These waterways also brought the Euro-Americans for furs, land, and inevitable conflict.

The U.S. Army built Fort Atkinson in 1820 to promote American trade with the Plains tribes, particularly along the Missouri River to the northwest. Later forts—Fort Kearny and Fort McPherson among them—protected the emigrant trails and the transcontinental railroad crews as they traveled west on the Great Platte River Road. Subsequent forts acted somewhat like police stations, patrolling and preserving an uneasy peace between the tribes and white settlement; these included posts like Fort Hartsuff, Fort Robinson, and Fort Niobrara.

Nebraska undoubtedly has the most developed "fort preservation program" of the Northern Plains, with four sites established as state parks and other sites serving as a community college, museums, and even a wildlife refuge. Many more fortifications are remembered through historical markers and monuments across the state.

Camp Clarke and Bridge   ★

BRIDGEPORT, MORRILL COUNTY

The discovery of gold by Custer's 1874 Black Hills Expedition meant the immediate need for an improved trail between the hills and the Union Pacific Railroad at Sidney, Nebraska. The biggest obstacle was the wide and shallow North Platte River. Entrepreneur Henry T. Clarke built a two-thousand-foot toll bridge across the stream in 1876, fully supported by the U.S. Army, with a small blockhouse on an island and troops stationed at its north end.

Traffic on the trail ended and the troops left by 1880 when railroads established service to the Black Hills. The bridge continued in use through the early 1900s but is gone today, with the river now running to the north of the site.

Location: A state historical marker and a DAR marker commemorate the camp and the bridge at a pull-off area, approximately 3.5 miles west of Bridgeport on U.S. Highway 26 (Nebraska 92). **GPS:** 41.670146°, -103.169018°.

This is where the scenic landmarks of the westbound trails started to appear. Courthouse and Jail Rocks are visible to the south; Chimney Rock, the most noted of landforms in emigrant diaries, is 10 miles further northwest on the same highway. A full interpretation of the land and trails is available at the **Chimney Rock National Historic Site**, managed by the state's historical society. The visitor center features a museum, interactive exhibits, and a gift shop; a newly established trail takes visitors to the base of the rock.

Location: Chimney Rock National Historic Site, 9822 County Road 75, Bayard, NE 69334. **GPS:** 41.702664°. -96.012603°.

Hours: Open daily from May 1 through October 1, 9:00 a.m. to 4:00 p.m. Off-season hours, Wednesday through Sunday, 9:00 a.m. to 4:00 p.m.

Admission: Fee charged

Phone: (308) 586-2581

Website: history.nebraska.gov/rock

Camp Lookout ★★

SIDNEY, CHEYENNE COUNTY

Indian attacks along the route of the Union Pacific's transcontinental railroad prompted the U.S. Army to send troops to Sidney in 1867 to protect work crews. The soldiers encamped on a rise north of the tracks overlooking the depot, building a two-story guard station from local limestone. The camp soon expanded to the south side of the tracks with the construction of Sidney Barracks.

The guard station survived over the years, becoming a hotel and then a private home (with alterations to its appearance). Recognizing its historical status as the oldest building in Sidney and probably the Nebraska Panhandle, a local group bought and restored the guard station to its original appearance.

Location: 940 Elm Street, Sidney NE 69162. **GPS:** 41.148765°, -102.976802°.
Hours: Tours are offered by appointment only; call to inquire.
Phone: (308) 254-5395
Website: www.sidneyboothill.com

44. A restoration returned the Camp Lookout guardhouse to its 1867 appearance.

Camp Sheridan ★

With the construction of the Spotted Tail Agency in northwest Nebraska in 1874 to supply treaty payments to the Brule Lakota, the Army built Camp Sheridan, named for Gen. Phil Sheridan, nearby to protect the agency. It was at the agency that Crazy Horse surrendered in 1877, and to Camp Sheridan that his parents brought his body after his killing at Camp Robinson on September 4. The following month the U.S. Army removed Spotted Tail's Brule to South Dakota and today's Rosebud Reservation; the army abandoned Camp Sheridan in 1881.

Location: A state historical marker in the Hay Springs city park (adjacent to U.S. Highway 20 on South Post Street) tells the brief history of the post and agency (**GPS:** 42.681886°, -102.692850°). To reach the actual sites, drive 1 block west of the sign to Beaver Road (County Road 1285) and follow the gravel road about 10 miles north to signs marking the location of both. **GPS:** Camp Sheridan: 42.850189, -102.735422; Spotted Tail Agency: 42.838574, -102.739810.

Fort Atkinson ★★★★

In their expedition to explore the Louisiana Purchase, Meriwether Lewis and William Clark met with Oto and Missouri Indians on a bluff overlooking the Missouri River in 1804. This first meeting with Plains Indians caused Clark to note in his journal that their "Council Bluff" and its commanding view of the valley made for an excellent fort or trading post site.

The U.S. Army built a temporary post north and below the bluff during the Yellowstone Expedition of 1819, but a deadly scurvy outbreak and a spring flood drove the troops to the bluff. They called the new post Camp Council Bluff or Fort Calhoun after U.S. Secretary of War John C. Calhoun but he ordered it named for the commander of the expedition and the post, Col. Henry Atkinson.

The fort protected the fur trade, kept peace with the Indians, and discouraged British forays into the area from Canada. It also hosted notable historical

45. Fort Atkinson's bluff site hosted the first meeting of Lewis and Clark with Plains Indians before the fort's construction.

figures like Col. Henry Leavenworth (its second commander), Gen. Stephen Watts Kearny, Jedediah Smith, Jim Bridger, Hugh Glass, Prince Paul the Duke of Wurttemberg, and Gen. William Harney.

Fort Atkinson quartered more than a thousand men in its garrison during the 1820s, representing almost a fourth of the nation's armed forces. With such a substantial number, it wasn't long before the fort's occupants realized they would need to grow their own food. Surprisingly, the so-called "Great American Desert" yielded great harvests. Gardens were plentiful at the site, and in 1822 the men husked almost nineteen-thousand bushels of corn to feed their cattle and hogs. A dairy at the post provided fresh milk and cheese.

Fort Atkinson's only military action came in 1823 after Arikara Indians attacked a trading party further up the Missouri River in what is now South Dakota. This "Arikara War" was a skirmish intended more to calm traders than to punish the tribe, but it was the first battle between U.S. troops and Plains Indians.

While General Atkinson (accompanied by a government Indian agent and a 435-man military escort) completed a series of peace conferences with tribes along the Missouri in 1825, a monstrous windstorm hit the fort and destroyed its mill. That and other expensive repairs, plus the government's

46. The Friends of Fort Atkinson present living history at the fort in the first full weekend of every month during the tourist season, including infantry drills.

interest in protecting the more active Santa Fe Trail, led to the fort's abandonment in 1827.

In 1961, local supporters bought the fort site and turned it over to the Nebraska Game and Parks Commission. Through state, private, and volunteer efforts, today's **Fort Atkinson State Historical Park** is an impressive reconstruction on the original site of the timbered fort, at one time the largest and westernmost U.S. Army post in the United States.

The first stop is at the newly updated visitor center-museum, which features displays on keel boating, earth lodges, mountain men, blacksmithing, the Louisiana Purchase, Lewis and Clark, and the War of 1812. Before walking through a grassy prairie to the fort, stop at the bronze sculpture garden depicting Lewis and Clark's meeting with the Oto and Missouri Indians. Reconstructions of the council house, the armory and blacksmith shop, and sutler's store, stocked with 1820s goods available for purchase, are beyond.

Inside the walls of the fort barracks is where you're surrounded by the 1820s fort experience. When the "Friends of Fort Atkinson" are in their reenactor roles during the summer months, give yourself at least three hours to fully enjoy the visit, not only for military drills and cannon fire, blacksmithing, and tinsmithing, but to smell the hot bread from the bakery, help the cooper create a barrel, or even assist the laundresses in doing the fort's wash.

Location: Fort Atkinson State Historical Park, 201 South Seventh Street,

Fort Calhoun NE, 68023. Eight miles north of 1-680, on the eastern edge of the town of Fort Calhoun; signs on U.S. Highway 75 will direct you to the park entrance. GPS: 41.452781°. -96.012603°.

Hours: Park grounds open daily at 8:00 a.m.; visitor center open daily from Memorial Day weekend to Labor Day, 10:00 a.m. to 5:00 p.m., and on weekends in May, September, and October (check website to confirm).

47. Fort Atkinson's blacksmith shop turns out items sold at the sutler's post.

Admission: Requires state park permit

Events: Historical reenactors present during the first full weekend of every month during the tourism season.

Amenities: Reconstructed fort, reenactments, historical markers, museum, gift and book shop, restrooms, hiking trails, and picnicking.

Phone: (402) 468-5611

Email: ngpc.Fort.Atkinson@nebraska.gov

Website: outdoornebraska.gov/fortatkinson/

Fort Butler

HEBRON, THAYER COUNTY

Responding to attacks in the area in 1869, the 1st Nebraska Cavalry's Company A built a small sod stockade along Spring Creek for settler protection. Named for then-Nebraska Governor David Butler, Fort Butler was never attacked, but its presence did lead to the establishment of the town of Hebron. The local DAR chapter placed a boulder and plaque in 1930 to commemorate this post.

Location: Northeast corner of 1st Street and Willard Avenue, Hebron NE. **GPS:** 40.158330°, -97.594685°.

Fort Garber

COMSTOCK, CUSTER COUNTY

Panicked setters of Douglas Grove built this small civilian post in the Middle Loup River valley during the agitated summer of 1876. They named the fort for Governor Silas Garber, but when an expected Lakota attack didn't come, the settlers gave it the moniker "Fort Disappointment." A brick monument stands west of the fort site.

Location: Located in eastern Custer County. From the town of Comstock, travel 1.3 miles west on Highway 21C and turn south on Oak Grove Road for 1.75 miles to the brick monument on the left. **GPS:** 41.528236°, -99.270109°.

Fort Hartsuff ★★★★

BURWELL, VALLEY COUNTY

One of the best-preserved forts of the Northern Plains and a prime example of the small prairie fort is Fort Hartsuff on the eastern edge of the Nebraska Sand Hills.

The Lakota were still here when homesteaders started streaming into the North Loup River valley for its fertile land. Skirmishes and the death of a settler brought calls for protection, and the friendly Pawnee at their nearby reservation also needed a buffer from their Lakota enemies. In September 1874 a military detachment established a Post on the North Loup, soon renamed for Maj. Gen. George L. Hartsuff who had died earlier in the year.

Area farmers were more than happy to become carpenters, masons, and haulers for Fort Hartsuff; grasshoppers wiped out their 1874 harvest and the fort's healthy construction budget of $110,000 ($3 million today) was needed income. The abundance of lime and gravel in the valley led to the new fort's buildings being constructed of grout, a type of concrete. For Fort Hartsuff's

48. One of the smaller prairie forts, Fort Hartsuff was a choice assignment for its quietness and social activities with local settlers.

49. Fort Hartsuff flies the thirty-seven-star U.S. flag, commemorating the number of states at the time of its founding in 1874. Coincidentally, its host state of Nebraska is the thirty-seventh state.

flagpole, the troops traveled much further—more than eighty miles to cut down a ninety-seven-foot pine tree at a tributary of the Niobrara River known as Pine Creek.

Fort Hartsuff was a choice assignment in the Department of the Platte. The pretty little post hosted events with local settlers, including a grand ball after the fort's completion, annual Fourth of July celebrations, dances, and other festivities. The fort continued to offer civilians work when times were hard—a farmer with his horse team could make three dollars a day hauling for the fort, and he always found willing customers for his produce.

The army rarely stationed more than fifty-five men at Fort Hartsuff. Patrols were their primary duty, but they also helped chase down horse thieves, murderers, robbers, and other frontier vermin. The only fight of any size was the Battle of the Blowout in April 1876 against a party of Lakota warriors a few miles northwest of the fort; one soldier was killed and three Medals of Honor awarded.

By 1880, however, the government confined the Lakota to the Dakota Territory with the new Fort Niobrara covering the territory's border with Nebraska. Fort Hartsuff's end soon followed with its abandonment in 1881 and sale of the fort to the Union Pacific Railroad for the incredible sum of $5,000—less than a *twentieth* of its construction cost just seven years earlier. The railroad planned a center to settle new emigrants to Nebraska, but instead sold the buildings and grounds to homesteaders.

A local optometrist bought the grounds to protect and restore the buildings, donating them in 1961 to the state of Nebraska for Fort Hartsuff's preservation and interpretation as a state park. Nebraska Game and Parks maintains today's **Fort Hartsuff State Historical Park** much as it was in the 1870s as one of the prettiest posts on the plains. White picket fencing connects the original buildings surrounding the parade ground, with stately trees shading the walk before the officers' quarters.

All nine of Fort Hartsuff's now-restored buildings survive to see their sesquicentennial (150th anniversary) in 2024. These include the post headquarters, enlisted men's barracks, officers' and commanding officer's quarters, post hospital, quartermaster storehouse, the quarters of the bakers, laundresses, and commissary sergeant, quartermaster stable, and guardhouse. Reconstructions at the site include the wagon scale, blacksmith-carpenter shop, and privy. All buildings are open with displays of furnishings and equipment from fort days.

The visitor center, located in the former post headquarters, includes interpretive displays and a gift shop, with books on the fort era and the region. During the summer, try to visit holiday weekends for the living history reenactors, performing the duties of soldiers, teamsters, and other personnel of the fort in the 1870s.

Location: Fort Hartsuff State Historical Park, 82034 Fort Avenue, Burwell, NE 68823. The park is 4 miles north-northeast of the town of Elyria on Highway 11, approximately 100 miles north of Grand Island exit 312 on I-80. **GPS:** 41.723242°, -99.023175°.

Hours: Most buildings open daily Memorial Day through Labor Day, 9:00 a.m. to 4:30 p.m. Visitor center and gift shop open daily in tourism season; off-season intermittently (call to confirm).

Admission: Requires state park permit

Amenities: Historical buildings and markers, tours (call in advance), museum, gift shop, restrooms, picnic area, occasional living history demonstrations.

Phone: (308) 346-4715

Email: ngpc.Fort.Hartsuff@nebraska.gov

Website: outdoornebraska.gov/forthartsuff/

Old Fort Kearny ★

NEBRASKA CITY, OTOE COUNTY

Brig. Gen. Stephen W. Kearny selected this site on the Missouri River near the mouth of Table Creek in 1846 as the first of a chain of forts to protect the overland trails. The Mexican-American War interrupted its construction and when building resumed, it was discovered the westward pioneers were crossing the Missouri farther to the south and to the north. The War Department soon relocated its troops in 1848 to the new Fort Childs on the Platte River, later renamed Fort Kearny. Old Fort Kearny became the beginnings of Nebraska City, with its blockhouse the site of the town's first printing press and newspaper. Local citizens marked the site in 1931 with a massive Sioux quartzite boulder.

Location: The boulder and plaque at Central Avenue and Fifth Street include a depiction of the blockhouse and commemoration of the Oregon Trail. There is also a state historical marker for Old Fort Kearny at the south-

50. Nebraska City's Old Fort "Kearney" monument reflects the confused spelling of Gen. Stephen Kearny's name.

east corner of Nuckolls Square Park, at 2nd Avenue and North 10th Street. **GPS**: Site Marker: 40.676405°, -95.851160°; State Historical Marker: 40.678612°, -95.857728°.

Fort Kearny

KEARNEY, KEARNEY COUNTY

While never among the most beautiful of the Great Plains military forts, Fort Kearny certainly was one of the most important and became one of the most historic. This small prairie fort anchored the eastern leg of the Great Platte River Road, and tens of thousands of people headed to Oregon, Utah, California, and Colorado came through here for supplies, repairs, communication, rest, and recovery.

Little of those essential services happened at the original location of Fort Kearny on the Missouri River, as that 1846 post proved too far from the Mormon and Oregon Trails to be useful. Its commander sent a detachment led by Lt. Daniel P. Woodbury to find a new site on the Platte in 1847. They came

51. Painting by William Henry Jackson of Fort Kearny (*right*) shows its location along the Platte River with the Oregon and California Trails in the foreground and the Mormon Trail dust clouds across the river. Courtesy National Park Service.

upon an elevated location about 180 miles west of the Missouri and a mile and a half south of the Platte with timber on the river islands, plenty of hay fields, and positioned between the warring tribes of the Lakota and Pawnee. Woodbury submitted the name of Fort Childs for the new post to honor Col. Thomas Childs of Mexican-American War fame and—coincidentally, of course—Woodbury's father-in-law.

The troops erected temporary sod structures while making adobe bricks and cutting timber for permanent buildings. Woodbury thought it important to plant trees on such a barren, treeless prairie, so cottonwoods were planted around the parade ground. The fort existed as Fort Childs for more than half a year, until the War Department ordered it renamed Fort Kearny to honor Gen. Steven W. Kearny after his death. (The city and county of Kearney are also named for the general, but under a common nineteenth-century misspelling of the name.)

The new Fort Kearny oversaw Oregon and Mormon Trail migrations, but the discovery of gold in California only intensified the rush past the fort. By 1849, the War Department reported that thirty thousand people had passed Fort Kearny in an eighteen-month period while on their way to Salt Lake and the west coast. The not-yet-famous passed through here, including newspa-

52. Fort Kearny's blacksmith shop is a reconstruction of the original sod structure at the fort.

per reporter Samuel L. Clemens (Mark Twain), U.S. Army Maj. Robert E. Lee, and army scout James Butler "Wild Bill" Hickok.

The fort expanded in size and scope, increasing its supply stores for the emigrants and the forts further west. The Pony Express had a station here (later a telegraph office), and regular stage and mail service made it one of the most crucial posts of the west.

That status continued through the Civil War but declined as the Indian Wars moved to the north and the west. Fort Kearny's last major function was in protecting work crews of the Union Pacific as they completed the transcontinental railroad; the fort closed in 1871 with the grounds opened to homesteading. More than fifty years later in 1928 an organization raised funds to buy and donate forty acres of Fort Kearny as park land to the state, which accepted it in 1929.

Today's **Fort Kearny State Historical Park** is a quiet, tall-treed stop for weary travelers from I-80. Entering the visitor center, take in the brief video on the park and its history and view nearly twenty-five displays covering the life and times of the fort and the people who used it. Dioramas of the fort through its various eras are particularly interesting. On the park's grounds, the stockade Fort Mitchel is a replica of a defense built during the Indian attacks of 1864. The grounds also include a blacksmith-carpenter shop reconstruction, stocked with the equipment and tools used at the time, and a reconstruction of the earthen powder magazine.

53. Artillery drills are a staple of Memorial Day weekends at Fort Kearny.

Your visit may coincide with a major update to the park. The Nebraska Game and Parks Commission is building a new visitor center, reconstructed officers' quarters and soldiers' barracks, as well adding improvements to the nearby Fort Kearny State Recreation Area.

Also, the city of Kearney is "the Sandhill Crane Capital of the World." If you can time your visit from late winter through early spring, you're on hand to see one of the planet's greatest natural migrations, as hundreds of thousands of these majestic birds congregate around the Platte River in their annual migratory pattern.

Location: Fort Kearny State Historical Park, 1020 V Road, Kearney NE 68847. Take I-80 to the Minden exit (exit 279), south on Highway 10 for 3 miles, then west onto Highway 50A for 3 miles. From the Kearney exit on I-80 (exit 272), south on Highway 44 for 2 miles, then east on Highway 50A for 4 miles. **GPS:** 40.641240°, -99.004886°.

Hours: Visitor center (which also serves as the Crane Information Center during migration season) open daily March 1 through April 15 and May 1 through September 30, 9:00 a.m. to 5:00 p.m.

Admission: Fee charged; requires state park permit

Amenities: Historic reconstructions and markers, visitor center and museum, gifts and books, restrooms, living history demonstrations Memorial Day weekend, Independence Day, Labor Day weekend. Nearby Fort Kearny State Recreation Area has camping, hiking trails, swimming, boating, fishing, and picnicking.

Phone: (308) 865-5305

Email: ngpc.Fort.Kearny@nebraska.gov

Website: outdoornebraska.gov/fortkearny/

Fort McPherson   ★★

The U.S. Army originally called the post built in 1863 east of the North Platte and South Platte Rivers' confluence Fort McKean, and it also went by the names Post of Cottonwood Springs and Fort Cottonwood. In 1866 the War Department officially named it Fort McPherson after Gen. James B. McPherson. This fort hosted five cavalry companies to protect the trails and rails, and William F. "Buffalo Bill" Cody, Gen. William Tecumseh Sherman, Gen. Philip Sheridan, and Lt. Col. George Custer all passed through its gates.

Fort McPherson was abandoned in 1880, but its cemetery—designated in 1873 as **Fort McPherson National Cemetery**—continued to host the burial of area Civil War veterans and the reinterred graves of soldiers from other forts in the Department of the Platte as they closed. Probably of most interest to today's students of the Plains Indian Wars is the Grattan Massacre monument, a large white marble memorial erected in the memory of Lt. John Lawrence Grattan and twenty-eight of his men who were killed near Fort Laramie in 1854; the monument and remains of the men were transferred here after the closure of Fort Laramie (Grattan is buried at Fort Leavenworth). Also from the Indian Wars are the graves of scouts Baptiste "Little Bat" Garnier and Moses "California Joe" Milner who fought with Kit Carson at Adobe Wells and scouted for Custer and Gen. George Crook. Spotted Horse, a Pawnee who fought white settlement but later served as a military scout, is also buried in the national cemetery, as are sixty-three Buffalo Soldiers of the 9th and 10th Cavalries, whose graves were removed from Fort Robinson.

About 1 mile southeast of the cemetery is a 1928 monument featuring a soldier at attention, marking the site of the flagstaff of the old military post. A small log cabin from the fort, probably a laundress's quarters, is located at the nearby **Lincoln County Historical Museum** (2403 North Buffalo Bill Avenue, North Platte NE 69101).

Location: Fort McPherson National Cemetery, 12004 South Spur 56A, Maxwell, NE 69151. Take exit 190 for Maxwell on I-80 and drive 4 miles south on Nebraska Spur 56A to the cemetery gate. GPS: National Cemetery: 41.024750°, -100.524523°; Flagpole Site: 41.016412°, -100.517836°.

Hours: The cemetery is open daily from dawn to dusk; closed federal holidays except Memorial Day.

54. A lone monument marks the flagpole site of the former Fort McPherson.

55. Now buried at Fort McPherson National Cemetery in their third mass grave—after the original battlefield and the cemetery at Fort Laramie—are the soldiers killed at the Grattan Fight. The incident was the opening event of the nearly forty-year Great Sioux War.

Fort Mitchell

SCOTTSBLUFF, SCOTTS BLUFF COUNTY

Troopers from the 11th Ohio Cavalry built this small post in 1864 west of Devil's Gap at Scott's Bluff, a towering natural landmark named for mountain man Hiram Scott whose remains were buried here in 1829. The troopers named Camp Shuman for their captain, Jacob S. Shuman. It was later named Fort Mitchell for district commander Brig. Gen. Robert B. Mitchell, while Devil's Gap was renamed Mitchell Pass. Constructed of sod and adobe complimented by a log corral, Fort Mitchell was a sub-post of Fort Laramie. Its troops saw limited action, helping in the defense of Mud Springs Station and in a skirmish near Horse Creek, both in 1865. The post was abandoned in 1867 and its adobe walls soon disappeared. A highway project in 2003 led to the discovery of artifacts and the fort site, where historical markers now stand. Besides Fort Mitchell, also disappearing over time was the apostrophe from Scott's Bluff; the landmark, county, and National Park Service site are today "Scotts Bluff," while the nearby city is Scottsbluff.

56. William Henry Jackson's painting of Fort Mitchell in 1867, with Scotts Bluff visible on the horizon.

Location: The markers for Fort Mitchell, as well as for the Oregon Trail and Pony Express, are 2 miles west of the city of Scottsbluff on a Nebraska Highway 92 pull-off area, adjacent to the fort site and the North Platte River. You can also take the scenic route to the marker on the Old Oregon Trail route from Gering northwest through Mitchell Pass and the scenic Scotts Bluff. **GPS:** 41.865593°, -103.727591°.

There are no additional amenities at the site, but Fort Mitchell is remembered with a display and diorama at the nearby **Scotts Bluff National Monument**. Besides the amazing history of the Oregon, Mormon, and Pony Express Trails through Scotts Bluff, the site features information on the geology, paleontology, wildlife, and flora of the area, and a stunning drive to the summit of the bluff.

Location: 190276 Old Oregon Trail, Gering NE 69341. **GPS:** 41.828402°, -103.707482°.

Hours: Open daily, 9:00 a.m. to 5:30 p.m. during tourism season, 9:00 a.m. to 4:00 p.m. in off-season; closed for major holidays.

Admission: Free

Phone: (308) 436-4340

Website: www.nps.gov/scbl/

Fort Niobrara

VALENTINE, CHERRY COUNTY

Named for the river it overlooks, Fort Niobrara was built in 1880 to police the Lakota reservations in the Dakota Territory, white settlements in Nebraska, and horse thieves and cattle rustlers in the northern Sandhills. Constructed toward the end of the Indian wars, its life was quiet, such as sending troops for a show of force in the Johnson County War in Wyoming between large cattlemen and small ranchers. Troops from the fort performed the same duty during the large-scale Pullman rail strike.

Fort Niobrara closed in 1906. It was used as a remount station for cavalry horses for the next five years, but closed permanently in 1911, with its buildings sold for scrap or moved. In 1912 the Department of the Interior established **Fort Niobrara National Wildlife Refuge** on the site to host a large herd of bison and elk; visitors can also enjoy plenty of natural attractions, such as scenic nature trails and the seventy-foot Fort Falls. The more adventurous can canoe the Niobrara, one of America's top canoeing rivers.

Location: Fort Niobrara National Wildlife Refuge, 39983 Refuge Road, Valentine NE 69201. About 4 miles east of Valentine on Highway 12. GPS: Wildlife Refuge: 42.893108°, -100.476689°; Historical Marker: 42.849751°, -100.534630°.

Hours: Grounds open sunrise to sunset; visitor center open Monday through Friday, 9:00 a.m. to 4:00 p.m.

Admission: Free

Amenities: Auto tours, wildlife watching, hiking, hunting, fishing, and canoeing.

Phone: (402) 376-3789

Website: fws.gov/refuge/fort-niobrara/

Fort O. K.

GRAND ISLAND, HALL COUNTY

During Indian attacks in 1864, Grand Island citizens fortified the town's O. K. Store with a sod stockade to protect the nearly 170 people sheltered there. General Samuel R. Curtis was so impressed with "Fort O. K." that he left a six-pounder cannon to defend against attacks, which never came. The barrel of the cannon stands on a monument dedicated by the DAR in 1939 at the Hall County Courthouse in Grand Island; there is also a historical marker to the O. K. Store at the state fairgrounds that describes the fort.

Location: The cannon monument is at the Hall County Courthouse, 111 West 1st Street, in downtown Grand Island; the state historical marker is at the Nebraska State Fairgrounds, 700 East Stolley Park Road, near the events center. GPS: Cannon: 40.923418°, -98.339632°; O. K. Store Marker: 40.904865°, -98.329187°.

57. The monument to Fort O. K. is perhaps the only monument of the Plains Indian Wars to contain an actual artifact of the wars—a six-pounder cannon donated for the fort's defense.

Fort Omaha   ★★★★

OMAHA, DOUGLAS COUNTY

Completion of the transcontinental railroad in 1869 meant the U.S. Army could close beleaguered forts on the frontier and instead ship men and supplies by rail to where they were needed. Sherman Barracks was built north of Omaha in 1868 with that strategy in mind.

Lt. Gen. William T. Sherman ordered his name removed from the small, forty-two-acre post of cheaply built barracks, and it thus became Omaha Barracks. Sherman compelled a name change once more in 1878 when—as General of the Army—he ordered all temporary posts be called "camps" and all permanent posts "forts." The army also moved the Department of the Platte headquarters from downtown Omaha to the new Fort Omaha in the orders.

Department commander Gen. George Crook and other officers joined in the move, making the fort a point of high interest for the elite of the city. Parties for the well-to-do always included the generals and other officers of

58. Today a community college library, the Fort Omaha Administration Building was later the fort's hospital with Walter Reed as one of its surgeons.

59. Ponca Chief Standing Bear. Courtesy Gilcrease Museum.

Fort Omaha, and the fort did its share of entertaining as well, including a visit by former president Ulysses S. Grant in 1879.

Another visitor—albeit unwilling—was Ponca Chief Standing Bear, who the U.S. government arrested and held at the fort in 1879 for leaving his Indian Territory reservation to return his dead son for burial in their Nebraska homeland. Crook carried out the arrest order but supported Standing Bear by encouraging a local newspaperman to rally support for the chief and by testifying on his behalf at the trial. The court's landmark ruling for Standing Bear represented the first time an Indian was recognized as a person under the law.

In 1894 the U.S. Army built Fort Crook near Bellevue to replace the much-smaller Fort Omaha, suspending operations at the latter in 1896. However, it reactivated Fort Omaha in 1905, adding new brick quarters and a signal corps school, followed in 1916 by a military balloon school. During World War II the fort served three roles: as a support installation for the 7th Service Command, as an army induction center, and as a work camp for Italian POWs. Command of the post was then handed over to the U.S. Navy; the last units of the Naval Reserve left in 1974 and the following year Fort Omaha was transferred to the Metropolitan Community College.

Today, flanked by busy city streets and fast-food restaurants at its doorstep, Fort Omaha is an urban oasis. Towering trees flank the parade ground and streets of the site, almost preventing visitors from admiring the commanding red brick buildings built in the fort's glory days. **General Crook's House**, built in 1879, stands as one of Omaha's few remaining examples of Italianate architecture. While the home's furnishings were not those of his and his wife's (few commanders brought furnishings with them to the frontier), what you'll see in the house is representative of the time they lived here. The Douglas County Historical Society maintains and operates the building as a museum, and it is well worth a visit.

Buildings along the tree-lined streets include the impressive Officer's Row, and about fifteen of them feature interpretive signs covering each building's role in the fort years. Virtually all structures are used by the community college, but their exteriors as well as the grounds are well maintained. A marker commemorating Standing Bear is on the northeast corner of the parade ground, across from the 1884 guardhouse.

Location: Fort Omaha Campus, Metropolitan Community College, 5730 North 30th Street, Omaha NE 68111. Fort Omaha is at 30th and Fort in north-

60. The General Crook House at Fort Omaha serves as the Douglas County Historical Museum.

east Omaha. From I-80, take I-480 to the North Freeway, following the highway until it spills onto 30th Street and the entrance of the iron-fenced campus. The Crook House is located at the northwest corner of the grounds. **GPS:** 41.308283°, -95.958789°.

Hours: Crook House: Monday through Friday, 10:00 a.m. to 4:00 p.m.; Saturday and Sunday, 1:00 to 4:00 p.m.

Admission: Fee charged

Phone: (402) 455-9990

Website: www.omahahistory.org

61. View of historic Fort Robinson, with the majestic Crow Butte on the horizon.

Fort Robinson

CRAWFORD, DAWES COUNTY

For the modern-day Plains Indian Wars traveler, if you were allowed to visit only one fort of the conflict, Fort Robinson *is* that fort. Often described as the crown jewel of the Nebraska state parks, Fort Robinson is the state's largest, most historic, and most scenic, with the surrounding forested buttes and canyons of the Pine Ridge. It's also the most visited, with nearly four hundred thousand visits every year, but don't expect it to be crowded on its twenty-two-thousand acres of wide-open, wild country.

It certainly wasn't a popular destination in 1873 when the U.S. government forced Red Cloud and his Oglala Lakota here from their original site on the North Platte River near Fort Laramie. Unrest and threats of violence from the tribe at the Red Cloud Agency led its agent to request military protection. Four companies of infantry and one of cavalry arrived at northwest Nebraska's Pine Ridge on March 5, 1874, to build Camp Robinson, named for Lt. Levi H. Robinson, killed in a skirmish near Laramie Peak the previous month.

The new camp provided security but did little to establish peace. Oglala Lakota were openly hostile to whites. They fired on Camp Robinson when the post's troops attempted to arrest a fugitive at the agency, and warfare nearly erupted when the white Indian agent decided to fly the American flag over the agency despite objections by the chiefs.

Actions by the government elsewhere seemed destined to tear the uneasy peace apart. The 1874 Custer expedition's discovery of gold in the Black Hills led to a rush into the Lakota's sacred lands. Soldiers from Camp Robinson

62. Red Cloud, ca. 1880. Courtesy National Portrait Gallery, Smithsonian Institution.

tried to evict the prospectors and the government offered to buy the Black Hills, but both efforts failed. The Lakota's refusal to sell in 1875 led to war the following year.

1876 was, of course, when the Oglala and other Lakota bands and tribes of the Plains annihilated Custer and his troops at Little Bighorn. Only three weeks after the battle had stunned and shocked the nation, around eight hundred Cheyenne left the Red Cloud Agency with plans to join their brethren who had fought against Custer. Col. Wesley Merritt and 350 troopers successfully intercepted them at Warbonnet Creek 25 miles northwest of Camp Robinson. The brief skirmish culminated in the Indians fleeing back to the agency and the death of well-known warrior Yellow Hair at the hands of Buffalo Bill Cody.

The most dynamic chapter of Fort Robinson came in 1877 with the surrender and death of Crazy Horse. Realizing he was being taken to the guardhouse rather than to council with post officials, Crazy Horse drew a knife and slashed out. In the ensuing scuffle with both a friend and guards, the Oglala leader was mortally wounded and died in the post adjutant's office. Although controversy persists, it is generally accepted that Crazy Horse died of a bayonet wound inflicted by the guard.

63. The reconstruction of the Fort Robinson guardhouse marks the site of Crazy Horse's death in 1877.

Camp Robinson's most tragic tale was told in 1879. Troopers apprehended and held several hundred Northern Cheyenne here after they attempted to return to their home in Montana, rather than live in forced exile on the Cheyenne reservation in Oklahoma. Refusing to comply with the government, 150 Cheyenne men, women, and children, led by Chief Dull Knife, shot their way out of Camp Robinson and ran for the buttes. The epic and tragic Cheyenne Outbreak lasted about two weeks in January of 1879, with cold, hunger, and constant pursuit by post troops leading to the deaths of some and the eventual surrender of the Indians.

Prior to the Cheyenne Outbreak, in December of 1878 Camp Robinson received word from the War Department of its designation as Fort Robinson to reflect its long-term, permanent status. When the Cheyenne left in 1879, however, Fort Robinson's role in the Indian Wars ended. Although it was only five years old, the fort certainly saw some of the Plains Indian conflicts' most dramatic and historic events.

"Fort Rob" continued to add to its history. The African American 9th Cavalry "Buffalo Soldiers" made the post their home in the 1880s, as did famed surgeon Dr. Walter Reed (his third fort assignment in Nebraska after Fort Omaha and Fort Sidney). The fort's troops weren't at Wounded Knee in 1890, but they were the first to be sent to the Pine Ridge Reservation during the Ghost Dance movement.

Fort Robinson became one of the more popular assignments in the early 1900s, especially for those loving the equestrian life. Its fox hunts and polo games lead some to call Fort Robinson the "Country Club of the U.S. Army." During World War II, the fort served as a training post for dogs in the K-9 Corps and as a German prisoner of war camp. The postwar mechanized army no longer needed horses, however, and turned Fort Robinson over to the Department of Agriculture in 1947 for use as a research station. The state of Nebraska gained a special-use permit for the original buildings in 1957, bought seventy-four acres of the old post in 1962, and in 1972 took over the remaining buildings and military reservation for use in the state park.

If you're traveling with family, you won't hear any whines of "there's nothing to do" when you're at **Fort Robinson State Park**. For the historian, there are the Fort Robinson History Center, original buildings, the post museum, and numerous historic sites marked on the grounds and in the surrounding area. The naturalist and the photographer will enjoy the stunningly beautiful Pine Ridge with its diverse wildlife, plant life, and scenic drives. For the geol-

64. The former post headquarters is today's Fort Robinson History Center.

ogist, there are nearby Toadstool Geologic Park, Agate Fossil Beds National Monument, and Fort Robinson's Trailside Museum.

For recreational lovers, there are stagecoach rides, Jeep rides, trail rides, rodeo games, melodramas at the post playhouse, and a nightly buffalo stew cookout. For the more active and outdoorsy types, there is canoeing, kayaking, golfing, hiking, biking, swimming, hunting and fishing. There's even something for the paleo-archeologist at the Hudson-Meng Bison Kill Site, a prehistoric bison hunt from nine thousand years ago. To make sure you don't miss a thing, you can take up lodging in one of the historic officers' or enlisted men's quarters. The casual visitor will spend most of a day, but one could easily spend a week.

Location: Fort Robinson State Park, 3200 Highway 20, Crawford NE 69339 (3 miles west of Crawford). **GPS:** 42.667353°, -103.466195°.

Hours: The Fort Robinson Inn and Lodge lobby is open 24 hours from Memorial Day through Labor Day for lodging and camping registration. The Fort Robinson History Center is open daily, May 1 through October 1, 9:00 a.m. to 4:00 p.m. and by appointment in the off-season.

Admission: Fee charged for museum; entry requires state park permit

Amenities: Lodging; modern or primitive camping; picnicking; fishing; restaurant; museums and visitor center; meeting and conference space; Jeep, hayrack, stagecoach, and nature rides; youth activities; golfing; swimming; hiking, biking, and horse trails; canoeing and kayaking; and concessions.

Phone: State Park: (308) 665-2900; Fort Robinson History Center: (308) 665-2919

Email: State Park: ngpc.Fort.Robinson@nebraska.gov; Fort Robinson History Center: hn.fortrob@nebraska.gov

Website: State Park: outdoornebraska.gov/fortrobinson/; Fort Robinson History Center: history.nebraska.gov/fort-robinson-history-center/

Nearby sites: Several historic sites surround Fort Robinson relating to the Indian Wars. About 1.75 miles west of the fort on Highway 20 is a state marker commemorating events of the **Cheyenne Outbreak**; another three-quarters of a mile west is a monument created by the Cheyenne people to the outbreak's casualties and survivors.

In the Crawford City Park (First and Main) is a 1912 monument for the **1876 treaty signing** between the Manypenny Commission and the Oglala Lakota, featuring a photograph of Red Cloud. State markers are also located 8 miles east of Crawford on Highway 20. Two miles north of those markers is the site of the **1875 Allison Commission treaty** negotiations (route is clearly marked).

Finally, the site of the **Warbonnet Creek Battle** is located 23 miles north of the fort. From Crawford, travel Highway 2 (Highway 71) north to the South Dakota border, then take Hat Creek Road south and west for 9 miles. GPS: 42.922735°, -103.729599°.

Fort Sidney

SIDNEY, CHEYENNE COUNTY

The quiet streets of today's Sidney hide the wild, dangerous, and often deadly past of the town, fueled in large part by the railroad and the army. The Union Pacific established Sidney in 1867 to support the transcontinental railroad construction, and the army simultaneously built Camp Lookout (page 89) to protect Union Pacific's men and equipment. The expanded camp, named Sidney Barracks, was a sub-post to Fort Sedgwick at Julesburg, but it wasn't long before it surpassed its Colorado parent.

The presence of soldiers, rail workers, gold seekers, freighters, gamblers, trappers, pioneers, and gunmen—all kept well lubricated by scores of saloons—turned Sidney into one of the wildest towns in the West. Sometimes the enlisted men were victims of the Wild West lifestyle. One was shot dead at a roadhouse dance—revelers simply moved him to a corner so the festivities could continue, and two more bodies joined his before the night was done.

Sidney Barracks increased in importance in the 1870s as a receiving depot for freight shipped to the northern forts and Indian agencies, and its soldiers became escorts for some of the larger bull trains on the trail. Units at the post were sent for duty in 1876 on the Yellowstone Expedition and the Powder River Expedition, and the fort was also a staging area for army forces sent to intercept Cheyenne bands breaking from their Oklahoma reservations.

In 1878 the War Department renamed the barracks Fort Sidney to reflect its permanence. The 1880s were peaceful, however, even more so when the fort and Union Pacific ran out the town's outlaws in 1882. Fort Sidney sent troops to South Dakota during the Ghost Dance movement and in 1891 to assist after the Wounded Knee massacre. The need for Fort Sidney concluded soon after. The post was abandoned in 1894 and the buildings were sold at auction in 1899. The town absorbed the fort's grounds and most of its forty buildings disappeared over the years.

65. The 1884 officers' quarters of Fort Sidney is home of the Cheyenne County Historical Museum in Sidney.

Besides the Camp Lookout guard station, at least three structures from Fort Sidney survive, all owned and maintained by the **Cheyenne County Historical Society and Museum**. The 1884 Officer's Quarters serves as the society's museum with a small exhibit on the fort; the nearby 1871 Commanding Officer's Quarters (1153 Sixth Avenue) is restored and outfitted for the nineteenth century; an octagonal 1872 powder magazine stands south of Fifth Avenue and Jackson.

Location: Cheyenne County Historical Museum, 544 Jackson Street, Sidney NE 69162. **GPS:** Museum: 41.144069°, -102.971767°.

Hours: Open May 1 through Labor Day, Monday through Saturday, 9:00 to 11:00 a.m. and 1:00 to 3:00 p.m., Sunday, 1:00 to 4:00 p.m.

Admission: Free

Amenities: Original buildings, tours, gift shop, and restrooms.

Phone: (308) 254-2150

Omaha Quartermaster Depot

OMAHA, DOUGLAS COUNTY

The first Omaha Quartermaster Depot, or "Government Corral," went up in 1866 on Union Pacific Railroad land at 13th and Webster in Omaha to supply the U.S. Army's frontier forts with horses, mules, equipment, foodstuffs, and other supplies. It was later moved to Fort Omaha and finally in 1880 to a triangular plot of five acres along the railroad's main line.

Even though by 1880 horses were no longer corralled at the new Omaha Quartermaster Depot, it couldn't give up the nickname of "the Old Corral." The depot served the Department of the Platte until the latter was phased out in 1898, but it continued to supply the surviving forts from the department, such as Fort Niobrara in Nebraska and Fort D. A. Russell in Wyoming. Brick buildings went up to replace wooden ones, and additional land increased its size to seven acres. The depot shipped millions of tons of supplies for the U.S. Army during World War I.

After failing to sell the depot as surplus after the war, the government used the installation as a transient shelter, equipment storage for the Civilian Conservation Corps, a World War II recruiting depot, an ordnance school for officers, an automotive training center, and an Italian POW camp. After

66. The Omaha Quartermaster Depot's 1880 Administration Building with the downtown Omaha skyline in the distance.

the war, the Old Corral garrisoned various units of the U.S. Army, the U.S. Army Reserve, and the Nebraska National Guard. The U.S. Army Corps of Engineers used one of the buildings as offices when their Missouri River offices were flooded in 2011. The government finally sold the property in 2014, with spaces now leased out for businesses.

Location: The depot, listed on the National Register of Historic Places, is south of downtown Omaha at South 21st and Woolworth. No building tours but the grounds are open for viewing. **GPS:** 41.244738°, -95.943442°.

Post Millalas ★

LEXINGTON, DAWSON COUNTY

Post Millalas was one of several former Pony Express and stage stations fortified and garrisoned during Indian attacks along the overland trails in 1864 and 1865. Named for stage station manager and rancher Patrick Mullally, his name somehow became "Millalas" when submitted and mentioned in dispatches. The temporary sod fort included officer's quarters, barracks, and stables, and is recognized by a granite marker near the site.

67. This private home is the former officers' quarters from the 1867 Post North Platte Station and likely the city's oldest building.

Location: Take exit 237 for Darr Road from I-80, head south on Road 755 for almost one and a quarter mile, and turn left onto Road 427. About a quarter-mile south is a pull-off area with markers for Post Millilas, the Oregon Trail, and the Willow Island Pony Express station. GPS: 40.767821°, -99.862897°.

Post North Platte Station

NORTH PLATTE, LINCOLN COUNTY

The War Department authorized a small military post at the new settlement of North Platte in 1867 to respond to area Indian attacks. Post North Platte Station protected the railroad bridge and depot in town, as well as Indians allied to the United States. Declining raids in Nebraska by 1878 brought the post's closure and the sale of its buildings in 1881. The officers' quarters survives today as a private home and is likely the oldest building in North Platte.

Location: The quarters (private home) is at 314 West Sixth Street in North Platte, west of downtown North Platte. GPS: 41.138796°, -100.766022°.

Post Plum Creek

HOLDREGE, PHELPS COUNTY

Built in September 1864 after the nearby Plum Creek Massacre, Post Plum Creek was one of the largest of the temporary posts constructed near the overland trails. The sod stockade fort had walls enclosing six buildings in a 325 square feet compound. It served as an intermediate station between Fort Kearny and Fort McPherson, hosting three companies of the 1st Nebraska Cavalry and two companies of ex-Confederate POWs now fighting for the U.S. Army (often called "galvanized Yankees"). It was abandoned in 1866 and is today marked by signage at the Plum Creek Cemetery.

   Location: Take exit 428 for Overton on I-80 and drive south on Spur 24B (Road 444). Cross the Platte River and turn right (west) at the "T" onto Road 748. After about 2 miles you'll reach the marked Plum Creek Massacre site, and in another 1.5 miles you'll reach the Plum Creek Cemetery and Post Plum Creek site. **GPS:** 40.672929°, -99.605733°.

Post South Loup Fork

RAVENNA, BUFFALO COUNTY

A sod sub-post of Fort Kearny, Post South Loup Fork was built in May 1865 by Company E of the 7th Iowa Cavalry to monitor the Lakota in the area. They were replaced by Company E of the 1st Nebraska Cavalry in July, and then the post was abandoned in August. In its short existence, the post also had the name Post Connor after Gen. Patrick Connor, "Fort Desolation" for its remoteness, and "Fort Banishment" by soldiers who saw service there as unfair punishment. A state historical marker commemorates the post.

   Location: The marker is at the north edge of Buffalo County, 1 mile east of Ravenna on Nebraska Highway 2, with the South Fork of the Loup River between the town and the marker. **GPS:** 41.010671°, -98.895588°.

U.S. Blockhouse ★

TEKAMAH, BURT COUNTY

A perceived Indian threat in 1855 led the new community of Tekamah to ask the Nebraska territorial government for aid and protection. The governor sent Gen. John M. Thayer of the territorial militia to organize a company and build a two-story, forty-by-forty-foot blockhouse in July 1856. The Indian threat never appeared, and the structure became a hotel and courthouse for at least the next ten years before it was torn down. A large monument at the Burt County Courthouse in Tekamah identifies the blockhouse as being built by the U.S. War Department (and the fort is traditionally called the "U.S." Blockhouse), but history indicates otherwise.

Location: Burt County Courthouse, 111 North 13th Street, Tekamah NE 68061 **GPS:** 41.778733°, -96.220817°.

68. Marker to the U.S. Blockhouse and other county sites and events at the Burt County Courthouse in Tekamah.

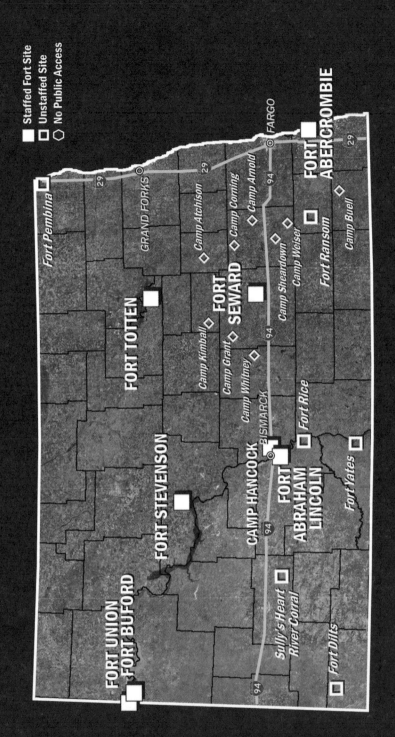

Legend:
- ■ Staffed Fort Site
- □ Unstaffed Site
- ⬡ No Public Access

FORT ABERCROMBIE

FARGO

29

29

Fort Pembina

GRAND FORKS

29

Camp Atchison

Camp Corning

Camp Arnold

94

Camp Sheardown

Camp Weiser

Fort Ransom

Camp Buell

FORT TOTTEN

FORT SEWARD

Camp Kimball

Camp Grant

Camp Whitney

94

FORT STEVENSON

BISMARCK

Fort Rice

CAMP HANCOCK

FORT ABRAHAM LINCOLN

Fort Yates

94

FORT UNION
FORT BUFORD

Sully's Heart River Corral

Fort Dilts

94

6. Forts of North Dakota

FORTS OF NORTH DAKOTA

The northern Great Plains was home to several nomadic and semi-nomadic tribes for generations before the arrival of the Euro-Americans. They included the Dakota and Lakota of the Sioux peoples, and the Mandan, Hidatsa, and Arikara. The vast grasslands of the Plains hosted millions of bison (or buffalo, as commonly known) which sustained the tribes with meat, hides for clothing and shelter, and bones and sinew for tools and weapons. The rivers and lakes of the land provided water and fish, with the Missouri River serving as a major transportation route.

The forts of North Dakota were built for the common reasons of the Plains—to control the tribes and enforce treaties, and to protect trails, rails, or settlements. The first military fort in today's state was Fort Abercrombie in 1858, built to protect settlers in the valley of the Red River of the North; somewhat ironically, it was one of the few forts to be attacked by native peoples in the history of the Plains Wars, this during the 1862 Dakota Uprising.

Forts from the 1860s had various purposes: Fort Buford protected the gold trail, Fort Rice supplied expeditions, Fort Stevenson protected the tribes from each other, and Fort Totten protected settlements. Fort Seward and Fort Abraham Lincoln of the 1870s protected the Northern Pacific Railroad construction, but the latter (with Lt. Col. George A. Custer heading the post) organized expeditions and campaigns, including Custer's ill-fated Little Bighorn Campaign of 1876.

North Dakota has a wonderful historic record of forts, with Forts Abercrombie, Abraham Lincoln, Buford, Stevenson, Totten and more all part of the state system, and Fort Union Trading Post is a National Park Service property, helping to tell the state's story of military posts.

Bad Lands Cantonment   ★

MEDORA, BILLINGS COUNTY, MONTANA

The Bad Lands Cantonment began in November 1879 as a small tent camp to protect Northern Pacific Railroad construction workers in the Medora area of the Little Missouri River. Eventually the tents were replaced by eight wood buildings and hosted up to sixty soldiers. Troopers saw little action during its existence through 1883, other than a brief engagement in June 1880 in which their horses were frightened, ran into the Indians' herd, and were captured, forcing the soldiers to walk the twelve miles back to the cantonment.

Some of Bad Land Cantonment's buildings later served Medora as its first school and newspaper offices. The site today is a modern campground, where a pull-off area has an historical display on the camp, the frontier military, and the one-time town of Little Missouri.

Location: Pull-off is in front of the Medora Campground, 3370 Pool Drive, Medora ND 58645. **GPS:** 46.9176°, -103.5333°.

Camp Hancock

BISMARCK, BURLEIGH COUNTY

This small infantry post began in 1872 as Camp Greeley, named for newspaper editor Horace Greeley, famous for saying, "Go west, young man." That name lasted for a little more than a year until October 1873 when the War Department changed its name to Camp Hancock for Gen. Winfield Scott Hancock, commander of the Department of Dakota.

The troops built Camp Hancock to protect the crew, supplies, and equipment of the Northern Pacific Railroad during its construction through the Dakota Territory. Within a decade, it also served as a quartermaster storage warehouse for shipping supplies by rail, wagon, or steamboat to western forts.

Starting in 1874, Camp Hancock became a Signal Corps reporting station to transmit military dispatches. Frontline troops were withdrawn from Camp Hancock in 1877, but it continued as a Signal Corps post until abandonment in 1894. The U.S. Weather Bureau took over the site, occupying it for the next forty-five years.

The State Historical Society of North Dakota acquired the site in 1951 and

69. Camp Hancock's 1872 officers' quarters in downtown Bismarck.

established the **Camp Hancock State Historical Site**, opening a museum in the original 1872 officer's quarters in 1955. A retired 1909 Northern Pacific locomotive later joined the site and the oldest church in Bismarck was moved here in 1965.

Location: Camp Hancock State Historical Site, 101 East Main Street, Bismarck ND 58501. **GPS:** 46.805291°, -100.790298°.

Hours: Museum open in summer Friday through Sunday, 1:00 to 5:00 p.m.; open by appointment only during winter; grounds open year-round.

Admission: Free

Amenities: Museum, original buildings, picnic area, restrooms, and tourism information.

Phone: (701) 328-9528

Email: shsfgm@nd.gov

Website: history.nd.gov/historicsites/hancock/

A more comprehensive telling of the state's Plains Indian Wars experience is found in the nearby **North Dakota Heritage Center and State Museum,** adjacent to the North Dakota State Capitol. This is the state's largest museum and features four galleries tracing its earliest geologic formation six hundred million years ago to today.

Location: 612 East Boulevard Avenue, Bismarck, ND 58505. **GPS:** 46.819182°, -100.778805°.

Hours: Open Monday through Friday, 8:00 a.m. to 5:00 p.m., Saturday through Sunday, 10:00 a.m. to 5:00 p.m.

Admission: Free

Amenities: Museum exhibits, events, café, gift shop, and restrooms.

Phone: (701) 328-2666

Email: history@nd.gov

Website: statemuseum.nd.gov

Fort Abercrombie

ABERCROMBIE, RICHLAND COUNTY

One of North Dakota's first state parks, Fort Abercrombie State Historic Site is also one of the few fort sites on the northern Plains to be attacked.

Lt. Col. John J. Abercrombie selected a site on August 28, 1858, on the west bank of the Red River of the North to protect settlers of the region, along with river and trail transportation, but flooding caused the fort's relocation to higher ground in 1860.

Fort Abercrombie was "the gateway to the Dakotas" for the pioneers and shippers from Minnesota to points west. It was the starting point for navigation down the Red River to Fort Garry (today's Winnipeg) in Canada and the terminal for military expeditions to the west. The post enjoyed a peaceful first few years, but events in 1862 threatened its very existence.

Word arrived on August 23 of the Dakota Uprising at the Redwood Agency and Fort Ridgely in Minnesota. Fort Abercrombie immediately ordered all soldiers to remain near the post, and settlers were advised to come to the fort for protection. The Dakota arrived August 30 and drove off the fort's livestock. A direct attack on the fort came September 3 and was repeated three days later. Army reinforcements finally arrived September 23, but that didn't prevent an additional attack six days later. The firing of a couple shells dispersed the warriors and the long siege of Fort Abercrombie ended. A stockade wall and blockhouses were soon added.

70. Fort Abercrombie's guardhouse, the fort's only original structure.

71. WPA reconstruction of a Fort Abercrombie blockhouse.

The fort played a part in the Indian Wars in 1863, receiving the sick and wounded from the Sibley Expedition against the Sioux. It protected military supply wagon trains, stagecoach routes, and steamboat traffic on the Red River, and served as a supply base for two major gold-seeking expeditions into Montana. When the rails came, Fort Abercrombie began protecting rail crews and keeping peace between local Indian tribes. It served as the hub for military mail routes from Fort Stevenson via Fort Totten and from Fort Wadsworth (Sisseton) via Fort Ransom.

The War Department ordered the post abandoned in 1877 and sold the lands and buildings. The town of Abercrombie soon formed a half-mile to the west. Its citizens kept the memory of the fort alive, buying the site and seeing its dedication in 1903 as one of North Dakota's first state parks.

The first stop at **Fort Abercrombie State Historic Site** is the modern information center, with a design evoking the park's WPA-era blockhouse replicas. Its museum shares the exciting history of the fort through displays and artifacts, and its observation deck provides an expansive view of the post's grounds and its setting on the Red River.

A ghosted stockade reconstruction marks the original perimeter of the fort. Besides the blockhouse reconstructions are the fort's original guardhouse,

72. Broadway Street from the town of Abercrombie actually courses through Fort Abercrombie State Historical Site before crossing the Red River into Minnesota. Green grassy areas mark the sites of original fort structures.

returned and restored after years at a nearby farm. You can walk through the structures, and the northeast blockhouse overlooks the Red River and the Minnesota shoreline.

Location: Fort Abercrombie State Historical Site, 935 Broadway, Abercrombie ND 58001. From I-29 exit 37, travel east for 6 miles along Richland County Road 4 through Abercrombie to the east edge of the town. **GPS:** 46.444825°, -96.718494°.

Hours: The fort grounds are open year-round. The interpretation center is open daily Memorial Day through Labor Day, 9:00 a.m. to 5:00 p.m., and by appointment only in the off-season.

Admission: Free to site; fee charged to museum and exhibits

Amenities: Interpretive center, museum and gift shop, reconstructed and original buildings, restrooms, guided and self-guided tours.

Events: Fort Abercrombie hosts living history events for Memorial Day, Flag Day, Aber Days (the local community celebration in June each year), Independence Day, and Labor Day weekend.

Phone: (701) 553-8513

Email: shsaber@nd.gov

Website: history.nd.gov/historicsites/abercrombie

Fort Abraham Lincoln   ★★★★

MANDAN, MORTON COUNTY

Like many forts, Fort Abraham Lincoln on the Missouri River evolved into something different than planned, but here was the possibly the biggest and fastest change of any American fort in terms of name, personnel, location, and construction.

In June 1872, Lt. Col. Daniel Huston selected a bluff near the Heart River's confluence with the Missouri to build an infantry post to protect engineers and labor crews building the nearby Northern Pacific Railroad. Blockhouses defended the post, named Fort McKeen for Col. Henry Boyd McKeen, killed in the Battle of Cold Harbor.

When department commander Gen. Phil Sheridan arrived, he found little to like about Huston's decision. He wasn't happy with the bluff site and its exposure to the high winds of the Dakota plains, and so ordered that fort improvements cease, that the base of operations move to the flatland below

73. Fort Abraham Lincoln State Park on the Missouri River.

the bluffs, and that cavalry become an essential part of the post. He authorized the renaming of the fort to Fort Abraham Lincoln in November in
memory of the assassinated president.

Infantry stayed on the bluff as the grounds below became home to cavalry
companies in the fall of 1873, including the 7th Cavalry led by Lt. Col. (Bvt.
Gen.) George Armstrong Custer. Custer became post commander and for
that reason it became known for many years as the "Custer Post." Quarters
and stables went up quickly, and by 1874 it was the largest and most important post of the Northern Plains, with around 650 infantry and cavalry soldiers. Custer organized his 1874 expedition to the Black Hills here, and it was
from the fort on May 17, 1876, that Custer and his entire command departed
for their rendezvous with destiny at Little Bighorn. There were 260 cavalry
troopers who left Fort Abraham Lincoln with Custer for the greatest of all
Plains Indian battles, most of whom never returned.

After returning from the Little Bighorn campaign, Gen. Alfred Terry organized a force of about 1,200 at the fort to continue punitive efforts against
the Indians, with remnants of the 7th Cavalry participating in the 1877 Nez
Pierce War in Montana. Troops protected the work crews of the Northern
Pacific, but once the railroad was completed in 1883 the need for the post
declined rapidly. The army closed Fort Abraham Lincoln in 1891.

The federal government transferred the property to the state in 1907. Original buildings were long gone, but redevelopment occurred in 1934 when the
Civilian Conservation Corps (CCC) built a museum and replica earth lodges,
blockhouses, shelters, and roads, and placed cornerstones to mark locations

of the original buildings at both fort sites. The site became part of the North Dakota Parks and Recreation Department in 1965.

Today's **Fort Abraham Lincoln State Park** still has the CCC structures, including three blockhouses at the Fort McKeen site and a spectacular view of the Missouri River valley and the capital city of Bismarck. The cavalry reconstructions are on the low ground at the park near the entrance. The most photographed site is the Custer House, rebuilt to the original specifications of the home once occupied by the general and his wife, Libbie. Additional reconstructions around the original parade ground are the post granary, barracks, stable, and the post commissary, which also houses the park's gift shop.

Gen. Geo. A. Custer

74. Lt. Col. George Armstrong Custer. Courtesy National Park Service.

75. The state park's Custer House is the third iteration of the commander's quarters and the longest lasting.

Give yourself four hours for your visit to the fort, including the reconstruction of the On-A-Slant Village of the Mandan Indians from 1575 to 1781. The CCC-built earth lodges deteriorated over time, but they were reconstructed and are accessible as part of the interpretive tour.

Location: Fort Abraham Lincoln State Park, 4480 Fort Lincoln Road, Mandan ND 58554. Fort Abraham Lincoln State Park is 8 miles south of I-94 and 7 miles south of Mandan on North Dakota Highway 1806. **GPS:** 46.757749°, -100.846580°.

Hours: The state park grounds are open year-round from sunup to sundown; the visitor center is open daily from 9:00 a.m. to 5:00 p.m.; the commissary is open seasonally.

Admission: Vehicle entrance fee charged; interpretive passes required for Custer House, historic fort buildings, and Mandan Village

Amenities: Visitor center, museum, historic reconstructions, book and gift shop, concessions, tours, historic and interpretive markers, camping cabins, modern and primitive camping, campfire programs, hiking, fishing, horse

76. The Fort McKeen blockhouse reconstruction is a reminder of the first military post at Fort Abraham Lincoln.

and bike trails, water, comfort stations, picnicking, snowmobiling and ATV trails are nearby. Interpretative tours of the site are available by appointment only to groups of six or more.

Phone: (701) 667-6340

Email: falsp@nd.gov

Website: parkrec.nd.gov/fort-abraham-lincoln-state-park

Fort Buford

Fort Buford was another post needed by the frontier army to protect travelers through Lakota lands to the gold fields of Montana. After first considering the old fur-trading post of Fort Union (page 153) at the border of the Dakota and Montana territories, Lt. Col. William G. Rankin traveled down the Missouri River for 8 miles and found a plateau at its confluence with the Yellowstone River. He established the new fort on June 13, 1866, and named it for Maj. Gen. John Buford, a hero of Gettysburg.

Led by Sitting Bull, the Lakota began raids on and near the post almost immediately to drive the whites from their country, attacking work parties and preventing mail service from reaching the fort. Buford's twelve-pound cannons saw regular action in keeping the Lakota at bay.

When not defending the trail, troops were rebuilding their fort. Because they built Fort Buford with green cottonwood, the boards shrank in the dry

77. The restored 1871 Brotherton House, the site of Sitting Bull's surrender in 1881.

Dakota winds and made it a very cold first winter for the troops. The army bought and demolished Fort Union for materials to build a new fort, but the use of green wood, green adobe, and unskilled labor meant the fort had to be rebuilt again in 1871 and 1878.

Fort Buford stood at an historic, essential crossroads in the Plains Indian Wars. It escorted supplies for the Little Bighorn campaign and its surgeon, Dr. George E. Lord, was killed at the battle. It continued as a major supply center throughout the mid-1870s, and any man not on regular duty was at the riverside, loading and unloading ships and wagons.

In the late 1870s and early 1880s, the chiefs and their tribes began to surrender. Chief Joseph of the Nez Pierce and Gall of the Lakota turned themselves in at Fort Buford. In 1881, Sitting Bull himself came from self-imposed exile in Canada and surrendered at the fort with 186 Lakota. In the wars' last years, troops at Fort Buford protected Northern Pacific Railroad work crews and guarded railroad property during the 1894 Pullman Strike.

A dilapidated Fort Buford was abandoned in 1895 and most of the buildings were sold or demolished. The once-great fort was not forgotten, however, and in 1924 was named a state historic site. **Fort Buford State Historic Site** is still a quiet, lonely site. The modern **Missouri-Yellowstone Confluence Interpretive Center** is the visitor center for the fort, and includes displays on Lewis and Clark, the area's wildlife, its fur trade, Indian artifacts, and original art. Allow an hour to visit this impressive center and its gift and book shop.

The fort is a half-mile away, giving the visitor an option to drive or walk there. There are several original and reconstructed buildings as well as the post cemetery there that tell the story of Fort Buford, but the main stop is the 1871 commanding officer's quarters, also known as the Brotherton House. It was in this building that Sitting Bull passed his gun over to the commander of Fort Buford.

Location: Fort Buford State Historic Site, 15349 39th Lane NW, Williston ND 58801. From the town of Williston, drive west on North Dakota Highway 1804 for 22 miles to the small village of Buford and the signage for the fort and confluence center; drive south for 0.9 miles. **GPS:** 47.986747°, -104.000137°.

Hours: Buildings open Memorial Day weekend through Labor Day, 10:00 a.m. to 5:30 p.m.; grounds open year-round. The nearby Missouri-Yellowstone Confluence Interpretive Center is open year-round, but with limited hours; call or email to confirm.

Admission: Fee charged

Amenities: Original and reconstructed buildings, museum, tours, modern facilities, and picnic area.

Phone: (701) 572-9034

Email: shsbuford@nd.gov

Website: history.nd.gov/historicalsites/buford

78. Sitting Bull, ca. 1881. Courtesy National Portrait Gallery, Smithsonian Institution.

Fort Dilts ★

RHAME, BOWMAN COUNTY

Fort Dilts was *not* a military post—it was a life-or-death, circle-the-wagons fight of sixteen days by gold-seekers and convalescent soldiers against Sitting Bull's Hunkpapa Lakota. The train of ninety-seven wagons left Fort Ridgely, Minnesota, for the Montana and Idaho gold fields in August 1864, arriving at Fort Rice, Dakota Territory, before the month's end. Picking up a military escort, they continued west and on September 2 were attacked by Lakota warriors. Two days later the group found a slight rise on which to form a

79. The gravesite of Corp. Jefferson Dilts, the namesake of Fort Dilts.

defense. They circled the wagons and began building a sod wall, six-and-a-half feet tall and three hundred feet in diameter. While runners rushed back to Fort Rice for reinforcements, the remaining fifty men held off the Lakota for more than two weeks at Fort Dilts, named for Corp. Jefferson Dilts killed and buried there; seven more soldiers and a number of civilians were also killed before relief arrived on September 20.

North Dakota established **Fort Dilts State Historic Site** in 1932. Relatively undisturbed, it includes several grave markers, site markers, interpretive signs, wagon ruts, a flagpole, and visible signs of the original sod walls.

Location: About 8 miles northwest of Rhame. From the town, travel U.S. Highway 12 west for almost 4.5 miles, turn north on the gravel 162nd Avenue sw for 2.3 miles, then head west for 1.5 miles. **GPS:** 46.278289°, -103.776457°.

Fort Pembina   ★

Long a major fur trading site at the confluence of the Pembina River with the Red River, the first military troops came to the area in 1863 after the Dakota Uprising. The troops left in 1864 but the U.S. Army returned in 1870 to respond to tribal unrest in the area. They built Fort George H. Thomas, named for the "Rock of Chickamauga" in the Civil War, south of the confluence, but two months later renamed the post Fort Pembina. Its quiet existence ended in 1895 when a fire destroyed most of the fort, leading to its abandonment.

Location: A small metal sign on Old Highway 1, south of the entrance to the Pembina airport and on the east side of the road, indicates the site of the fort but has no additional information. **GPS:** 48.947916°, -97.238678°.

The **Pembina State Museum** (805 State Highway 59, Pembina ND 58271) has a display on Fort Pembina including artifacts from the site and one of the original military reservation markers. This modern museum tells the story of the native peoples, European traders, and Pembina's role as a gateway between the United States and Canada, the border of which is less than 2 miles away. Be sure to take a view of the Red River valley from the museum's seven-story observation tower.

Hours: Open daily in tourism season and Tuesday through Saturday in the off-season.

Admission: Free, nominal charge for tower

Amenities: Museum store, travel information, and restrooms.

Phone: (701) 825-6840

Email: shspembina@nd.gov

Website: history.nd.gov/historicsites/Pembina

Fort Ransom ★★

FORT RANSOM, RANSOM COUNTY

The U.S. Army built Fort Ransom (named for Civil War general Thomas E. G. Ransom) in 1867 to protect immigrants from Minnesota heading to Montana. This was not a plum assignment—behind its log-and-sod breastwork were mostly unfinished single-story log structures with two log blockhouses completing the post. The nearest water was six hundred yards away, and hay for the animals was three miles away. During the fort's history, there were no deaths due to Indian attack, but five troopers died from natural causes and two Indian mail carriers froze to death on the trail.

Five years after its construction, Fort Ransom was obsolete. Materials from it were removed to construct Fort Seward in 1872, and the military reservation's land was sold to homesteaders. Today's **Fort Ransom State Historic Site** is also sparse; the small grassy park includes depressions marking the original buildings and the moat surrounding them. The entire site, along with the historical and interpretive markers that cover history and life at the fort, can easily be taken in within a half hour.

Location: The fort site is 0.6 miles southwest of the town of Fort Ransom. If driving from I-94 at Valley City, take the scenic county highway south at exit 292. **GPS:** 46.518794°, -97.941555°.

Hours: Open daily.

Admission: Free

Amenities: Historical and interpretive markers and parking. Camping and other amenities are available at Fort Ransom State Park, located 2 miles north of the town of Fort Ransom.

Phone: (701) 973-4331

Email: frsp@state.nd.us

Website: www.ndparks.com/Parks/FRSP

Fort Rice ★★

Gen. Alfred Sully established Fort Rice, named for Gen. James Clay Rice, killed in the Battle of Spotsylvania, in July 1864 during his expedition against the Dakota. The fort's stated purpose was to supply the expedition, but eventually was to control the native peoples, protect emigration from Minnesota to Montana, and protect navigation on the Missouri River.

Fort Rice was an operations base for both of Sully's expeditions. Important Indian councils were held at the fort from 1866 to 1868, including a great council with area Lakota that led to the Fort Laramie Treaty which ended Red Cloud's War. In the early 1870s, the fort served as the base for the first three Yellowstone expeditions. Four of Fort Rice's 7th Cavalry companies traveled with Custer on his 1874 Black Hills Expedition and two companies fought at Little Bighorn. By 1878, however, the newer Fort Yates served the region's needs and Fort Rice was abandoned.

80. In 1870, the House Committee on Military Affairs commissioned artist and retired army general Seth Eastman to paint seventeen important forts to commemorate the end of the Civil War. Eastman in 1873 painted Fort Rice, recognized for its protection of the Missouri River navigation during the conflict with the Dakota. Collection of the U.S. House of Representatives.

Today's **Fort Rice State Historic Site** is a somewhat stark site. There are no original buildings—just foundations of former structures on dry, hard ground, pockmarked by prairie dog mounds. Restrooms and parking are located at the site, but no other visitor amenities are available.

Location: Fort Rice is on Highway 1806, nearly 1 mile south of the town of Fort Rice, or 29 miles south of I-94 at Mandan. **GPS:** 46.512620°, -100.583408°.

Fort Seward   ★★

JAMESTOWN, STUTSMAN COUNTY

Named for U.S. Secretary of State William Seward and overlooking the James River valley, Fort Seward protected the Northern Pacific Railway's construction—not from area Indians but from rail workers who tore up the tracks if they weren't paid on time. The 1872 fort was also a base for Indian scouts, a depot for Fort Totten to the north, and protector of cattle herds en route to the Missouri River. Once railroad construction ended in 1877, the army abandoned Fort Seward, dismantled the buildings, and shipped the lumber to Fort Totten. The Northern Pacific, which owned most of the fort site, donated a portion of the land in 1925 to the State Historical Society.

The **Fort Seward Historic Site** is today owned by the city of Jamestown and includes picnic grounds and three historical markers. The state's largest American flag flies at the site as a city landmark. A small interpretive center includes a diorama of the fort, display cases of artifacts found in archeological digs at the fort, and a small gift section.

Location: Fort Seward Interpretive Center, 602 10th Avenue NW, Jamestown ND 59270. Look for the large American flag in the northwest end of Jamestown, as it is at the site of the fort. **GPS:** 46.913026°, -98.721015°.

Hours: Fort grounds open year-round; call to check hours for Interpretive Center.

Phone: (701) 251-1875

Fort Stevenson

Several fort sites on the Missouri River were lost with the damming of the river in the 1950s, but Fort Stevenson was one that enjoyed a bit of a rebirth because of it.

The first rendition began as a replacement to Fort Berthold in 1867 built to protect the Arikara, Mandan, and Hidatsa from the Lakota. Initially called New Fort Berthold, the War Department renamed it Fort Stevenson for Gen. Thomas G. Stevenson killed in the Battle of Spotsylvania in the Civil War. The fort protected river transportation, helped move mail between other forts, and supplied Fort Totten, 126 miles to the east.

In 1883, after its abandonment, Fort Stevenson became an Indian school through 1894. The Department of the Interior then sold the fort's buildings to local landowners, and in the 1950s came the Garrison Dam and Lake Sakakawea which swallowed up the grounds.

Today's **Fort Stevenson State Park** shares little more with its namesake than a reconstruction of the fort's unusual guardhouse, located on a bluff about 2 miles northeast of the original one and offering a fantastic view of Lake Sakakawea at its widest point. The building has multiple functions, but primarily serves as the visitor center and museum of the park. Among its displays are Indian and military artifacts, a scale model of the steamboat Far West (which brought news to the fort of Little Bighorn), and a cross-section recreation of the fort's thick adobe walls. Featured in the museum is Gen. Philippe Regis de Trobriand, commander of the fort in its first two years. His paintings and sketches created during his Fort Stevenson days are on display—in fact, it was his detailed notes that allowed the accurate reconstruction of the guardhouse.

Location: Fort Stevenson State Park, 1252A 41st Avenue NW, Garrison ND 58540. Situated 4 miles south of Garrison on County Road 15, overlooking Lake Sakakawea. **GPS:** 47.588118°, -101.420827°.

Hours: The Fort Stevenson museum is open daily, Memorial Day through Labor Day, from 10:00 a.m. to 7:00 p.m.; open off-season by appointment.

Admission: Requires state park permit

Amenities: Visitor center, museum, historic building reconstruction, gift shop and bookstore, research library, camping cabins, modern and primi-

81. An inexact reproduction of the Fort Stevenson guardhouse hosts the museum and visitor center on the shore of Lake Sakakawea.

82. Gen. Philippe Régis de Trobriand. Courtesy National Portrait Gallery, Smithsonian Institution, Frederick Hill Meserve Collection.

tive camping, marinas, concessions, hiking and biking trails, cross-country skiing, picnicking, modern restrooms, playgrounds, swimming beach, dog park, and rentals.

Special Events: Frontier Military Days is held the fourth weekend of June to give visitors the chance to experience life at an 1870s military fort.

Phone: (701) 337-5576

Email: fssp@state.nd.us

Website: parkrec.nd.gov/fort-stevenson-state-park

Fort Totten ★★★★

FORT TOTTEN, BENTON COUNTY

The Army built the first Fort Totten in 1867 on the south shore of Devils Lake as a small log-and-mud fort. But as the border with British Canada to the north was still insecure and a certain amount of "peacekeeping" was needed to protect settlement in the region, work on a larger fort began almost immediately. Bricks were cast from clay taken from the foot of Sully's Hill

83. One of the few Northern Plains forts that still has most of its original structures, Fort Totten requires constant preservation efforts against the Devils Lake climate.

and eventually the soldiers built thirty-two structures, twenty-four of which were brick.

Devils Lake and the rolling, timbered hills made Fort Totten an attractive assignment and it was peaceful as well, with no battles at or near the surrounding Cut Head, Wahpeton, and Sisseton Sioux reservation. But isolation and weather could be harsh, and alcoholism was frequent.

The Battle of the Little Bighorn hit Fort Totten hard. Two-thirds of the men under the direct command of Lt. Col. George Armstrong Custer were stationed at Fort Totten and called back to Fort Abraham Lincoln shortly before they marched out to Montana. Maj. Marcus Reno briefly commanded the fort in 1874. Dr. James DeWolf, post surgeon for both Forts Totten and Seward, was killed at the battle, as was Capt. Miles Keogh, stationed at Fort Totten before his transfer to Fort Abraham Lincoln.

Fort Totten's role as a fort ended in 1890 as the government's Indian policy moved from annihilation to assimilation. The federal government took Indian children from their families and placed them in boarding schools to learn the ways of the whites. A local Indian school operated at the old fort through 1935 when Fort Totten first became a tuberculosis preventorium and then a vocational school. In 1945 the vocational component ended and the fort became a community school under the independent Spirit Lake tribal government. The school was moved off the fort site in 1959, and in 1960 the federal government transferred Fort Totten to the State Historical Society of North Dakota.

With sixteen maintained buildings, **Fort Totten State Historic Site** is the best-preserved military post of the Dakota frontier era, a testament to the state historical society's efforts given the harshness of the Devils Lake climate on the buildings. Each building has two small signs identifying its historic role during the fort days and the school days.

One of the most striking differences between Fort Totten and other North Dakota forts is the abundance of shade trees on the parade ground. When established, the post was very much part of the "treeless plains" as early photographs reflect. After the War Department directed the planting of trees at the forts in 1871, the policy was thoroughly embraced at Fort Totten and continued by school children for Arbor Day.

A trip to Fort Totten is a two-to three-hour visit. Starting with the commissary and visitor center, you can take in a study of area photographs and artifacts from the fort's history, a scale model of the fort, and replica of a fort's

commissary interior. A visit can be extended, as the captain and first lieutenant's quarters are today's Totten Trail Historic Inn, a bed and breakfast.

Location: Fort Totten State Historical Site, 417 Cavalry Circle, Fort Totten
ND 58335. Fort Totten is 86 miles north of I-94 (exit 258) and 101 miles west of
I-29 (exit 141) on the Spirit Lake Reservation, near North Dakota Highway 57
and just south of the agency town of Fort Totten. **GPS:** 47.977316°, -98.993891°.

Hours: Buildings open from Memorial Day through Labor Day, 9:00 a.m.
to 5:00 p.m.; open weekdays in off-season by appointment. Grounds open
year-round, 9:00 a.m. to 5:00 p.m. weekdays.

Admission: Fee charged

Amenities: Original buildings, museum, lodging, restrooms, interpretive
center, and gift shop.

Phone: (701) 766-4441

Email: shstotten@nd.gov

Website: history.nd.gov/historicsites/totten

Fort Union ★★★★

WILLISTON, WILLIAMS COUNTY

Like its sister National Park Service property Fort Laramie (page 208), Fort
Union began its life on the Plains as a trading post for the Native American
and European American peoples. Fur trader Kenneth McKenzie built the
fort at the confluence of the Missouri and Yellowstone Rivers for the American Fur Company in 1828, serving as its first bourgeois, or superintendent.
It featured a solid stockade around its buildings that housed employees,
furs, food stores, and other supplies; other structures included shops for the
blacksmith and tinner, stables, icehouse, and powder magazine. The Bourgeois House, a beautiful ornate structure that served as McKenzie's home,
dominated the grounds.

Fort Union itself dominated the area trade with the Blackfeet (who had
previously refused to trade with Americans) and the Crow, further increasing
McKenzie's regional power and influence. He employed nearly a hundred at
times in the summer and perhaps a fourth of that in the winter. Many were
from foreign lands and ancestry—artisans of all types walked its grounds,
and those who were married had married Indian women (no white women

84. Fort Union's position below the confluence of the Missouri and Yellowstone Rivers brought it great prominence as a trading post before its brief time as a military post.

85. The reconstruction of the Fort Union gate—showing the peaceful interaction between native peoples and white Euro-Americans—welcomes the visitor into the fort's trade area and Bourgeois House.

had lived there during its entire history). For the most part, it was an era of goodwill between whites and Indians.

Alcoholism and smallpox plagued Fort Union's trading partners, however, leading to a great number of deaths. Those issues and changes in the fur trade inevitably led to the Lakota replacing the original tribes of the area and the decline of trade at the fort. The U.S. government used the fort to distribute annuities for some of the tribes starting in the 1830s. Gen. Alfred Sully reached Fort Union in late 1864 and found the fort dilapidated, but his troops stayed there through the winter.

The army built Fort Buford (page 140) in 1866 and dismantled Fort Union for materials. The Great Northern Railroad placed a flagpole at the fort site in 1925 to commemorate its position on the rail line. The state of North Dakota named it a state historical site in 1941, holding it until 1966 when the National Park Service took over the grass-covered grounds for excavation and found the sites of the palisades, the Bourgeois House, and many other buildings. A reconstruction of Fort Union began in 1985 including its walls, stone bastions, the Indian trade house, and the Bourgeois House.

Fort Union Trading Post National Historic Site is one of the most impressive of the fort sites of the Northern Plains. The rugged scenery of the west-

86. Fort Union's ornate Bourgeois House, home of the trading post superintendent and now the National Park Service site's visitor center and museum.

ern North Dakota–eastern Montana region is already appealing, but to enter an open plateau and find this small, almost castle-like fortress with its white walls and red shingled roofs on the banks of the Missouri is inspiring. The National Park Service has purposely kept the land around the reconstructed post clear of modern structures so, apart from some cropland, visitors enjoy an authentic nineteenth-century view of the post.

To enter the fort, you'll pass under a recreation of the original painting showing the peaceful trade and interaction between Indians and whites. The main attraction—the Bourgeois House—is straight ahead. This colorful two-story reconstruction serves as the visitor center and museum for the historic site.

To your left is the sod-roofed trade house where trade was conducted with the various tribes and where the bourgeois sometimes met with important chiefs. To the far left is the site of the dwelling range, a long house which sheltered clerks, traders, laborers, and their families; to the far right is the site of the storage range that housed the retail store, storage room for the trade goods, and the fur and buffalo robe storage room. Plan to spend at least two hours at Fort Union.

Location: Fort Union Trading Post National Historical Site, 15550 Hwy 1804, Williston ND 58801. From Williston take U.S. Highway 2 west to North Dakota 1804, turn left, follow 1804 past Fort Buford and 2 miles past Highway 58 to the park entrance. From Sidney, Montana, take Highway 200 north to its intersection with Highway 201 in Fairview; cross into North Dakota and take Highway 58 north to the park. **GPS:** 47.999274°, -104.040657°.

Hours: Open daily, 9:00 a.m. to 5:30 p.m.; closed Thanksgiving, Christmas, and New Year's Day.

Admission: Free

Amenities: Visitor center, museum, historic building reconstruction, gift shop and bookstore, picnicking, modern restrooms, water, and walking trails.

Special Events: The Fort Union Rendezvous, held the third weekend in June, features more than a hundred reenactors demonstrating traditional skills and lifeways. The Indian Arts Festival over the first weekend of August features the traditional arts and crafts of the Northern Plains tribes, along with storytelling, weapon crafting, flint knapping, and more.

Phone: (701) 572-9083

Email: fous_Superintendent@nps.gov

Website: nps.gov/fous/

Fort Yates ★

After establishing the Standing Rock Agency in 1873, the U.S. Army built Post Standing Rock Agency the following year to protect the agency and the Yanktonai, Hunkpapa, and Blackfeet. The reservation was a hotbed of unrest, since the tribes were sending men and supplies to Sitting Bull before the Battle of the Little Bighorn. The post also provided troops and supplies to the Little Bighorn campaign and was renamed Fort Yates in 1878 for Capt. George Yates of the 7th Cavalry, killed at the battle.

Fort Yates figured prominently in Old West history. Sitting Bull was returned to the agency from imprisonment at Fort Randall in 1883, and U.S. Indian Police left from Fort Yates to arrest Sitting Bull during the Ghost Dance agitation in 1890. After the police killed the great chief during their failed arrest, they brought his body to Fort Yates for burial. The army deactivated the fort in 1895, with its last troops leaving in 1903. Only the post's 1870s guardhouse stands today. The **Sitting Bull Burial Site and Memorial** is just north of Yates Street and clearly seen at your entry into Fort Yates; interpretation and picnic tables are available.

Location: The Missouri River town of Fort Yates covers the original fort site today; the guardhouse (closed to the public) is at the southeast corner of Cottonwood Street and Proposal Avenue. **GPS:** 46.091497°, -100.629865°.

87. Fort Yates's former guardhouse.

Sully's Heart River Corral ★

RICHARDTON, STARK COUNTY

Gen. Alfred Sully established this site on the Heart River as a base camp on July 26, 1864, holding surplus supplies and equipment here as well as a wagon

88. The site of Gen. Alfred Sully's base camp on the Heart River, marked by the State Historical Society of North Dakota.

train of immigrants while he continued his expedition against the Dakota. That campaign resulted in a crushing attack on a Lakota encampment at Killdeer Mountain on July 28, although these people were not involved in Minnesota's Dakota Uprising. Sully returned to the corral on July 31 and moved his column on to the Yellowstone River. The State Historical Society of North Dakota erected a granite monument and plaque here in 1955 to mark the site.

Location: Drive 12.5 miles south of the Richardton exit off I-94 on State Highway 8. Turn left (east) on 50th Street sw for 7 miles, and 0.6 miles north on 81st Avenue sw. The marker is in a pasture, 660 feet east of the road. GPS: 46.696740°, -102.153303°.

The Sibley Camps

EASTERN NORTH DAKOTA

Many Minnesotans feared more attacks or wanted retribution following the Dakota Uprising of 1862, even though the Indians had retreated into the Dakota Territory. Gen. John Pope, commander of the Department of the Northwest, wanted to trap the Dakota there. He called for Col. Henry H. Sibley to march to Devils Lake, Gen. Alfred Sully to move up the Missouri River valley, and for both to capture or kill any Dakota caught between the two before they rendezvoused on July 25.

Although the 1863 expeditions were successful, they didn't go according to plan. Sibley made rapid pursuit through the territory from late June through mid-August, engaging the Dakota at Big Mound, Dead Buffalo Lake, and Stony Lake. Sully's command was hit by numerous delays including a change in command, delayed steamboats, and delayed regiments, causing him to miss the rendezvous with Sibley. Sully attacked the remaining Dakota at the Battle of Whitestone Hill on September 3, devastating the tribe before winter.

Sibley's march resulted in a series of military encampments commemorated by the State Historical Society of North Dakota as state historic sites. That designation gives the impression that these are developed sites; rather, many of these camps are in remote, rural areas accessed by gravel, sometimes dirt roads, with no amenities. Be advised of weather and road conditions before visiting.

89. The marker for Camp Sheardown, one of many temporary encampments established during Col. Henry Sibley's 1863 punitive campaign against the Dakota.

Camp Arnold: Includes the headstones of two soldiers who died and were buried in camp. Four miles north of Oriska in Barnes County along Highway 32, on the west side of the road at a field entrance. **GPS:** 46.993273°, -97.791186°.

Camp Atchison: Fieldstone monument and aluminum marker at a pull-off, almost 3 miles southeast of Binford, Griggs County, on Highway 1. GPS: 47.524066°, -98.329267°.

Camp Buell: Fieldstone monument and aluminum marker at a pull-off at the west edge of Milnor (Sargent County) on State Highway 13. GPS: 46.248812°, -97.456818°.

Camp Corning: A granite marker indicates the site, 6 miles east of Dazey (Barnes County) on State Highway 26 and 2 miles north on gravel County Road 19 to its intersection with 14th Street SE; marker is on the northeast corner. GPS: 47.212090°, -98.067736°.

Camp Grant: A granite boulder and plaque mark the camp. From Woodsworth in Stutsman County, travel west 1 mile on State Highway 36, north for 3 miles on the gravel 55th Avenue SE, and west 1.75 miles on 16th Street SE to the boulder. GPS: 47.182974°, -99.371891°.

Camp Kimball: From Carrington in Foster County, take State Highway 52 west for 4 miles, turn south on gravel 62nd Avenue SE for 4 miles, west for a quarter-mile on 1st Street SE, south for 1 mile on 62nd Avenue SE, and east for .8 miles on dirt road 2nd Street SE to the unmarked site. GPS: 47.384704°, -99.206255°.

Camp Sheardown: Marked by a boulder from the local DAR chapter. From Valley City in Barnes County, on the south side of I-94, take 8th Avenue SE east to the gravel 118th Avenue SE. Follow the road for nearly 1.75 miles south to the forced left turn (east); the boulder is another quarter-mile on the south side of the road. GPS: 46.891300°, -97.970366°.

Camp Weiser: A small granite marker surrounded by a split rail fence denotes the site. From Kathryn, Barnes County, travel east for 3.2 miles on gravel 51st Street SE and then go south for 2 miles on 122nd Avenue SE to a dirt road. The marker is 0.8 miles directly east but may not be accessible due to water levels. GPS: 46.644714°, -97.875366°.

Camp Whitney: The expedition camped here after the Battle of Big Mound on July 25 and buried regimental surgeon Dr. Josiah Weiser here, whose death started the battle. The Camp Whitney State Historical Site is unmarked at the end of a mile-long pasture road. Much easier to reach is the Big Mound Battlefield Overlook and Dr. Weiser's gravesite. Camp Site: Approximately 10 miles northeast of Tappen in Kidder County, nearly 1 mile north of 30th Street SE, 2.3 miles east of its intersection with 39th Avenue SE. **GPS**: 46.993136°, -99.588451°. Weiser Marker: Take 39th Avenue SE north from Tappen for 9 miles, turn east for 1 mile, then north for 1 mile, and finally west for one-half mile on 27th Street SE; the granite marker is one-tenth mile to the south in the field site and reads "Dr. J.S. Weiser Killed Here by the Sioux July 24, 1863" and sits atop a boulder. **GPS**: 47.022317°, -99.628895°.

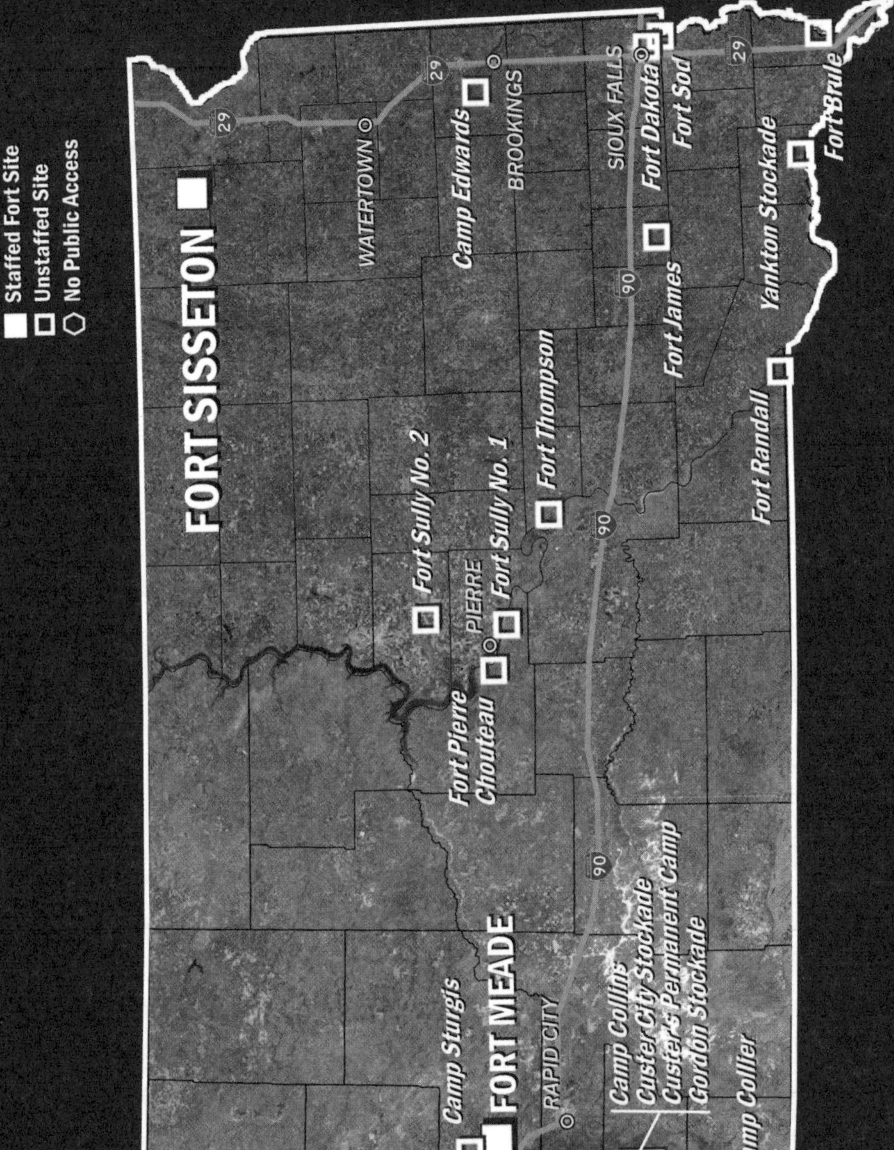

Legend:
- Staffed Fort Site (filled square)
- Unstaffed Site (open square)
- No Public Access (hexagon)

FORT SISSETON

29

WATERTOWN ⊙

Camp Edwards

BROOKINGS

29

SIOUX FALLS

Fort Dakota

Fort Sod

Yankton Stockade

Fort Brule

90

Fort James

Fort Thompson

Fort Randall

90

Fort Sully No. 2

Fort Sully No. 1

PIERRE ⊙

Fort Pierre Chouteau

90

Camp Sturgis

FORT MEADE

RAPID CITY ⊙

Camp Collins
Custer City Stockade
Custer's Permanent Camp
Gordon Stockade

Camp Collier

90

7. Forts of South Dakota

FORTS OF SOUTH DAKOTA

The Lakota Sioux—including the Oglala, Brule, and Hunkpapa bands—were among the more prominent tribes in the region of today's South Dakota, with the Dakota Sioux (Santee) and Cheyenne also a significant presence. They, too, shared the vast buffalo herds with other Plains tribes, but a natural resource that proved impossible to share between tribes and Euro-Americans were the Black Hills.

The federal government first established its presence in the region by taking over the fur trading post of Fort Pierre Chouteau in 1855; it soon proved substandard, leading to the first constructed military post of Fort Randall. Many of the forts built after that time—like Fort Sisseton—were built to protect white settlements, but others like Fort Meade were there to control the vast and numerous tribal reservations. Small civilian posts protected communities from farmers to gold panners.

Today, South Dakota has marked most of its military post sites, while only a few have original buildings, with Fort Meade using the former post headquarters as a museum. The main attraction is Fort Sisseton, however, with its fully restored buildings in a beautiful setting and an annual festival to celebrate its historic past.

Camp Collier ★

EDGEMONT, FALL RIVER COUNTY

Troopers from Company K, 4th Infantry out of Fort Laramie built Camp Collier (also known as Camp at the Mouth of the Red Canyon) in June 1876 as the first "permanent" military post of the Black Hills to protect travelers on the Cheyenne-Black Hills stage route. Named for Capt. William S. Collier, the stockade measured 125 square feet, large enough to host up to fifty-six men as its garrison, plus laundresses and their children. Camp Collier only lasted a year, however, when the stage took a shorter route through Hat Creek and Camp Jenny in today's Wyoming.

Location: A state historical marker to Camp Collier is located 3 miles northeast of Edgemont on U.S. Highway 18. **GPS:** 43.340815°, -103.782973°.

Camp Collins ★

CUSTER, CUSTER COUNTY

Naming it for a trader at Fort Laramie, Gen. George Crook established Camp G. H. Collins at the prospective Custer City in 1875 to ensure gold miners stayed out of the Black Hills. Toward that end, they also kicked out the non-native occupants of the new town and the camp's commander, Capt. Edwin Pollock, took over the unfinished cabin of Dr. Daniel W. Flick as his headquarters.

The camp disbanded in 1876 and Dr. Flick returned to reclaim his cabin, finding it finished and now occupied by noted scout and newspaper correspondent "Captain Jack" Crawford. The dispute over the cabin resulted in Custer County's first civil lawsuit and a win for the doctor. Flick lived in his cabin through about 1900 and it still stands today as South Dakota's oldest building, located between the 1881 Courthouse Museum and the current Custer County Courthouse.

Location: Way Park, South 4th Street and Mount Rushmore Road (U.S. Highway 16), Custer SD 57730. **GPS:** 43.765682°, -103.600981°.

90. The cabin of Dr. Flick became the post headquarters of Camp Collins in 1875, surviving today as South Dakota's oldest building.

Camp Edwards ★★

BRUCE, BROOKINGS COUNTY

This post—also known as Cantonment Oakwood—consisted of a single log hut surrounded by five-foot-high, one-hundred-foot-square breastworks. The 2nd U.S. Infantry built the camp in 1859 and occupied it during the 1862 Dakota Uprising; after the Civil War, the Minnesota Volunteer Cavalry temporarily stationed here.

The site is within Oakwood Lakes State Park, with a marker and an outline of the breastworks. There is also a state marker immediately west of Volga on U.S. Highway 14 which mentions the post.

Location: Oakwood Lakes State Park, 20247 Oakwood Drive, Bruce SD 57220. The marker is situated at the south end of Campground 2. **GPS:** Park: 44.442919°, -96.984327°; U.S. Highway 14 Marker: 44.326365°, -96.931383°.

Admission: Vehicle permit required

Amenities: Camping, boating, trails, restrooms, and picnic area.

91. Camp Sturgis—indicated by this highway marker—was located near the slopes of Bear Butte, standing in the distance.

Camp Sturgis ★

STURGIS, MEADE COUNTY

Camp Sturgis—named for Lt. James G. Sturgis, killed at the Battle of the Little Bighorn and son of 7th Cavalry regimental commander Lt. Col. Samuel D. Sturgis—was the 1878 temporary tent encampment of troopers building nearby Fort Meade. During the soldiers' two months there, they were customers of nearby "Grasshopper Jim" Frederick's store where they could count on being "scooped" or cleaned out by the shopkeeper. Scooptown became the store's nickname as well as that for the town of Sturgis after the soldiers moved to their permanent site.

Location: A state marker for Camp J. G. Sturgis and Scooptown is at the intersection of 130th Avenue (Highway 79) and 201st Street, northwest of the prominent Bear Butte. GPS: 44.488767°, -103.447466°.

Custer City Stockade

CUSTER, CUSTER COUNTY

A wooden marker at the Custer Post Office states that in 1876 citizens built a 100-by-150-foot log fort across the street for protection from Sioux Indians. No historical record is found of this defense, however, and local historians report town buildings would have been in the location. The marker may refer to a fort built for a 1920s film or a one-time tourist attraction that somehow became conflated with history.

   Location: U.S. Post Office, 643 Mount Rushmore Road, Custer SD 57730. **GPS:** 43.767310°, -103.597599°.

Custer's Permanent Camp

CUSTER, CUSTER COUNTY

The official mission of General Custer's Black Hills Expedition of 1874 was to find a fort site to subdue the Lakota; unofficially, the expedition would satisfy reports of considerable gold deposits in the hills. The expedition's prospectors on July 30 found small bits of gold in French Creek and more the next day. Custer decided to set up a "permanent" camp and sent word of the discovery to Fort Laramie via his scout Charley Reynolds.

   Also known as Agnes Park for Custer family friend Agnes Bates, the site has several markers. A state highway historical marker for the August 1–6, 1874 encampment is along the highway in front of an RV park. Another marker—built of native stone and with a plaque erroneously reading "General Custer Camped Here July 1874"—is about 250 yards north of her on Heller Road. (Next to this marker is the grave of Pvt. John Pommer, who died here of chronic diarrhea while on campaign with Crook in 1876). Finally, continuing to the northwest for another 250 yards, Custer, South Dakota author Paul Horsted placed a large all-weather sign near French Creek where the prospectors first found gold, which led to the camp's establishment.

   Location: Three miles east of Custer on U.S. Highway 16. **GPS:** Highway Marker: 43.770253°, -103.538463°; Stone Marker: 43.771673°, -103.538893°; Discovery of Gold Marker: 43.773024°, -103.540802°.

92. A granite marker erected by area residents shows the stockade construction of Fort Brule.

Fort Brule

RICHLAND, UNION COUNTY

Soldiers and settlers built Fort Brule during the Dakota Uprising of 1862, one of scores of civilian defenses built to protect citizens in the region. Its nine-foot stockade walls offered protection against attacks that never came, but Fort Brule succeeded in surviving beyond the conflict in the area as a temporary home for a dozen families, a recruiting post for the Dakota cavalry, and a church of sorts for Methodist services up to 1868. In 1937, citizens of the area erected a monument at the original site along the Brule Creek, showing a rendition of the fort and a brief history.

Location: Seven miles east of the rest stop at the intersection of I-29 and South Dakota Highway 50 on the north side of the highway. GPS: 42.761870°, -96.673815°.

Fort Dakota

SIOUX FALLS, MINNEHAHA COUNTY

Troops arrived in Sioux Falls in 1865 to build a small fort and convince people to move back to the area after the 1862 Dakota Uprising. First named Fort Brookings, the small, poorly built post of a few buildings was renamed Fort Dakota. Volunteers manned it but regular troops arrived in 1866 as Sioux Falls repopulated. It closed in 1869 and its men and material were sent to Fort Randall (page 176).

Location: A small plaque erected in 1941 by the DAR in downtown Sioux Falls commemorates Fort Dakota and is today located at the northeast corner of Eighth and Phillips; a half-block north on Phillips is a stand-alone marker placed by the county historical society. The fort stood across Phillips to the west. GPS: Plaque: 43.548755°, -96.726645°; Marker: 43.549280°, -96.726688°.

Note: Fort Sod site (included later in this chapter) is 2 blocks to the southeast.

Fort James ★

Named for the adjacent James River, this small fort was built in 1865 by the 6th Iowa Cavalry to garrison troops protecting stagecoaches and buffering white settlement from the Lakota. It lasted a year before its closing in fall 1866. In 2008 archaeologists with the Public Broadcasting Service TV program "Time Team America" made a three-day dig before placing a small, inscribed stone post to mark the fort site. The outlines of the stone walls are visible.

Location: East of the unincorporated Rockport Hutterite Colony, about 7.5 miles southwest of Alexandria. Drive south and past the colony on 418th Avenue until reaching cattle pens on your right; take the dirt road left (east) for a quarter-mile to reach the site, looking for the red stone post marker. **GPS:** 43.576899°, -97.835057°.

Fort Meade

For years the U.S. Army wanted a military post near Bear Butte, a 1,200-foot rocky rise to the northeast of the Black Hills. The butte flanked the main trail to the favorite hunting grounds of the Lakota and, in the 1870s, the trails from Bismarck, Fort Pierre, and Sidney to the gold fields of Lead and Deadwood.

The first post in 1878 was the temporary Camp Sturgis (page 168) with the permanent site founded later in the year, 5 miles to the southwest and roughly 14 miles from Deadwood. Maj. Gen. Phil Sheridan reportedly rode about the site, pointing with his sword where he wanted buildings. It was originally named Camp Ruhlen for Lt. George Ruhlen, who supervised the construction of the buildings, but then renamed Fort Meade for Maj. Gen. George G. Meade, commander of the Army of the Potomac at Gettysburg.

Lt. Col. Samuel D. Sturgis continued as the fort commander and invested in the nearby town that would bear his name. The 7th Cavalry was the first permanent garrison at the fort after troops reformed at Fort Abraham Lincoln following the Battle of the Little Bighorn.

The regiment brought two survivors back from the Little Bighorn to Fort Meade. Maj. Marcus A. Reno led the first charge at Little Bighorn and was blamed by many for Custer's defeat; a seemingly cursed life continued at the fort when Reno was charged with peeping through the window of Col. Sturgis's house at his commander's attractive daughter. Already awaiting trial for a barroom brawl at the Officers' Club, Reno was dishonorably discharged from the army in the court martial, ending his twenty-three-year career.

The second survivor was more highly revered. Comanche was the severely injured horse of the slain Capt. Miles Keogh and was exaggeratingly identified as the 7th Cavalry's "sole survivor" of the battle. He was nursed back to health at Fort Abraham Lincoln and traveled with the 7th to Fort Meade. He was never ridden and probably spoiled while at the fort and later at Fort Riley, Kansas.

Fort Meade was called the "peacekeeping post" and it largely lived up to the nickname as the last fort built in the Dakotas. It headquartered troops at Wounded Knee in 1890 and intercepted and hosted many Utes trying to

93. Fort Meade in 1888, with Bear Butte in the distance. Courtesy Library of Congress.

leave their Utah reservation for Canada in 1906. The fort saw military duty through both world wars and even served as a POW camp before the War Department turned it over to the Veterans Administration in 1944.

The site is now home to the Fort Meade Veterans Administration Medical Center, which you may not even see when visiting the historic original parade ground and buildings. Signs direct you to the **Old Fort Meade Museum** in the post headquarters where you'll view a video history of the fort before the self-guided tour. The museum features a wide variety of artifacts and displays such as those on Dewey Beard, the last Indian survivor of Little Bighorn, on Major Reno's "peeping" incident, the fort's involvement in World Wars I and II, Buffalo Soldiers, and the 7th Cavalry.

You can walk or drive around the old parade ground using the map provided by the museum. Among the many original buildings are the 1878 commissary (the first building built on the post), officers' and bachelor officers' quarters, and the Maj. Marcus Reno home (1879). The Fort Meade National Cemetery is on the hillside overlooking the fort.

94. Former post headquarters and present Fort Meade Museum.

Location: Old Fort Meade Museum, Building 55 Sheridan Street, Fort Meade, SD 57741. From I-90 in Sturgis, take exit 30 and Highway 34 2 miles east to Fort Meade. **GPS:** 44.410661°, -103.471364°.

Hours: Open mid-May to end of September, Tuesday through Saturday, 10:00 a.m. to 5:00 p.m.

Admission: Fee charged

Amenities: Historical buildings and markers, tours, museum, gift shop, bookstore, and restrooms.

Phone: (605) 347-9822

Email: info.oldfortmeade@gmail.com

Website: fortmeademuseum.org

Fort Pierre Chouteau

FORT PIERRE, STANLEY COUNTY

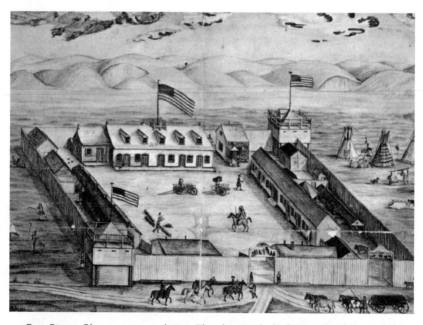

95. Fort Pierre Chouteau around 1854. This drawing belied the ramshackle condition Gen. William S. Harney found the fort in upon his arrival in November 1855. Courtesy National Archives.

Built in 1832, Fort Pierre Chouteau—or simply, Fort Pierre—was the most successful fur trading post on the upper Missouri River. The U.S. government bought the fort on reputation alone in 1855, not realizing that mice and fleas infested the site, termites had destroyed the stockade and buildings, and timber and grass surrounding the fort had been stripped away over the years. When Gen. William S. Harney arrived with his 450 soldiers in November following his victory at Ash Hollow in Nebraska, he found no provisions for sheltering his troops that winter. He abandoned the site the next year, moving downstream to a new Fort Randall. A 1930 granite marker and a small park with interpretation occupy the site today.

Location: **Fort Pierre Chouteau National Historic Landmark**, 348 Fort Chouteau Road, Fort Pierre SD. From Fort Pierre, take Highway 1806 north and drive for 1.3 miles to Fort Chouteau Road; turn east and follow the signs to the park. **GPS**: 44.391028°, -100.387618°.

Fort Randall

PICKSTOWN, CHARLES MIX COUNTY

Gen. William S. Harney's decisive 1855 defeat of the Brulés at Ash Hollow in Nebraska Territory pushed the major Lakota tribes to seek peace. Harney wanted a significant military presence to ensure that peace, and when Fort Pierre Chouteau proved unfit he selected a downstream site on the Missouri River and named it for Col. Daniel Randall, the late deputy paymaster general.

Fort Randall protected travelers on overland routes along the Platte River, settlers in the Missouri River valley, and refugees during the Minnesota outbreak in 1862. The U.S. Army completely rebuilt the fort in 1871, replacing the deteriorating one-story log structures with two-story wood frame buildings. Area residents pitched in to build a church for both communities. The attractive new buildings, white picket fences, and flower gardens made Fort Randall elegant and among the best constructed forts of the Northern Plains. By the 1880s, however, most of the Indian tribes were on reservations; Fort Randall was closed in 1892 and sold the buildings and surplus equipment at auction except for the church, which continued for years before its abandonment.

The 1950s construction of the Fort Randall Dam drastically changed the land around Fort Randall. Fortunately, its grounds lie before the dam rather than beneath Lake Francis Case. The U.S. Army Corps of Engineers' visitor

96. The sheltered ruins of the Fort Randall Church is the sole remaining structure of what was once one of the Northern Plains' most elegant forts.

center on the east side of the dam has a small display section on the fort, along with a view of the river and lake. The fort site is open to the public with interpretive signage for a self-guided tour. The only structure remaining are the ruins of the Fort Randall Church, sheltered by a modern roof to protect it from further deterioration.

Location: Fort Randall Military Post is 12 miles west of Wagner on South Dakota Highway 46, or 25 miles northeast of Spencer, Nebraska on U.S. Highway 281. **GPS:** 43.049362°, -98.562157°.

Hours: Visitor center open from Memorial Day through Labor Day, 8:00 a.m. to 5:30 p.m.; closed Tuesdays and Wednesdays.

Admission: Free

Amenities: Historical and interpretive markers, restrooms, and water are available at the fort site. Restrooms, displays, staff, picnic tables, and water are available at the visitor center. Modern camping is at the adjacent Randall Creek Recreation Area.

97. The historic North Barracks acts as the visitor center for today's Fort Sisseton.

Fort Sisseton

LAKE CITY, MARSHALL COUNTY

Possibly the most beautiful of the South Dakota forts and certainly the best preserved is Fort Sisseton of the Kettle Lake region. Prettiness wasn't the concern of Dakota Territory settlers of the area, however, after forced relocation of tribes to their region from the 1862 Dakota War in Minnesota. To calm their fears the U.S. Army in 1864 built Fort Wadsworth, named for Gen. James S. Wadsworth, killed earlier that year Battle of the Wilderness in the Civil War. The fort had plenty of fresh water from surrounding lakes, and abundant timber, clay, and limestone for building.

The new fort and the 1864 Sully and Sibley campaigns pacified most of the Lakota and Dakota in the region, but settlers were still nervous. An 1866 rumor of an Indian attack led Chief of Scouts Sam Brown to warn nearby camps of the impending danger, but after arriving at the first camp after five hours of hard riding he learned that the reports were false. He rode back to Fort Wadsworth to calm their fears but got caught in the dark and then rain, sleet, hail, snow and finally a classic Dakota blizzard. He made it back to the fort after his 150-mile ride but ended up partially paralyzed for the rest of his life due to exposure. He also picked up the nickname of "the prairie Paul Revere" from the misadventure.

98. Cavalry drilling during the annual Fort Sisseton Historical Festival.

Fort Wadsworth never saw an attack, but it was prepared. The fort employed more than two hundred Sisseton Lakota as scouts, stationed at camps throughout what is now southeast North Dakota and northeast South Dakota. The army renamed it Fort Sisseton in 1876 to honor the friendly tribe located at the reservation adjacent to the fort.

Activities at Fort Sisseton were more social than military, hosting far more suppers and balls than skirmishes and battles. The Indian scouts were released from service in 1881 but many continued to work at the post, catching deserters and arresting civilians who trespassed on the military reservation in search of timber. The fort was abandoned in 1889 and its buildings were used by the local community for social activities and later for lodging. Restoration efforts began on the old fort in the 1930s and Depression-era programs helped restore some buildings. In 1959 Fort Sisseton became a state park.

Fort Sisseton Historic State Park is one of those great sites that retains its original history in a picturesque setting with activities for the whole family. The visitor center in the former north barracks is your first stop, where you can view a short video on post history and a great display on life as a soldier. Other buildings are the carpenter and blacksmith's shop, stable, hospital, doctor's quarters, commanding officer's quarters, officers' quarters, adjutant's office, magazine, guardhouse, commissary sergeant's quarters, oil house, south barracks, and schoolhouse—again, all are original buildings, and most are open to the public. The only reconstruction is the log block-house at the northwest corner.

Throughout the summer, you'll encounter staff and volunteers in period clothing to give an even greater experience of life at Fort Sisseton, but the best time to visit is the first weekend in June when the Fort Sisseton Histor-ical Festival and V. M. Starr Rendezvous is in full swing. An encampment of cavalry, infantry, traders, and muzzleloaders are there to demonstrate a Gatling gun, cannon, and other period firearms while in authentic uniforms, tents, wagons, and field conditions of the period. A wide variety of activities are available, so don't leave anyone at home.

Location: Fort Sisseton Historic State Park, 11907 434th Avenue, Lake City SD 57247. From I-29 at Sisseton (exit 232), take Highway 10 west and drive 28 miles. The fort is 9 miles south of Highway 10 (roughly 10 miles south of Lake City). **GPS**: 45.657764°, -97.530603°.

Hours: Grounds open year-round; visitor center open daily, Memorial Day through Labor Day, 10:00 a.m. to 6:00 p.m.; check website for off-season hours.

Admission: Vehicle permit required

Amenities: Visitor center, museum, tours (call in advance), original build-ings, camping cabins, campground, gift shop, biking, hiking trails, horse trails, picnic shelters, canoeing, boating, and fishing.

Special Event: Fort Sisseton Historical Festival during first full weekend in June, featuring cavalry and infantry encampment and vendors.

Phone: (605) 448-5474

Email: FortSisseton@state.sd.us

Website: https://gfp.sd.gov/parks/detail/fort-sisseton-historic-state-park/

Fort Sod ★

SIOUX FALLS, MINNEHAHA COUNTY

Without the benefit of a treaty with the Yankton Lakota, land speculators from Iowa in 1856 crossed the Big Sioux River near its falls and staked out a town site. Men from Minnesota joined them the next year and merged their efforts to establish Sioux Falls City. The Yankton destroyed the nearby town of Medary in the summer of 1858, throwing Sioux Falls City into a panic. Citizens built a substantial sod stockade around the land company's stone building and hid behind the walls of "Fort Sod" for an attack that never came, although the Yankton did study the defense from a distance for three days.

Location: There are several historical markers commemorating the fort in downtown Sioux Falls, all within a block of each other. There is a 1928 DAR marker and modern interpretive marker next to a dog park at 201 South 2nd Avenue (**GPS:** 43.545880°, -96.724497°); a county-state historical marker to the "Incident at Fort Sod" 400 feet to the north at 111 East 9th Street (**GPS:** 43.546838°, -96.724940°); and a bronze plaque across River Road with other plaques on the riverfront (**GPS:** 43.547144°, -96.724806°).

Fort Sully No. 1

PIERRE, HUGHES COUNTY

Nearly sixty years after Lewis and Clark visited the site, Gen. Alfred Sully and his men established a fort to protect settlers on the east bank of the Missouri River in 1863. It was originally named for its first commander, Lt. Col. E. M. Bartlett, but the War Department soon renamed it for Sully.

99. Marker for the first Fort Sully at the Farm Island State Recreation Area.

The fort featured twelve-foot walls and blockhouses of cottonwood logs. It hosted a large treaty conference with Indians of the Upper Missouri in the fall of 1865, but its existence was short. Unhealthy conditions were rampant at the fort, with rats, mice, and fleas everywhere. It was abandoned in late summer 1866, with a new Fort Sully constructed about 30 miles upriver. The old fort was dismantled and used as steamboat fuel.

The site of Fort Sully is in today's Farm Island State Recreation Area, a large camping and boating area on the Missouri River south of the capital city of Pierre. The SRA's Lewis and Clark Family Center is within the fort perimeter, with small white markers embedded in the ground indicating the corners of the fort. Additional interpretation is in the family center, and there is a state historical marker on a Highway 34 pull-off south of the Farm Island entrance.

Location: Farm Island Recreation Area, 1301 Farm Island Road, Pierre, SD 57501. Located 4 miles south of Pierre on South Dakota Highway 34, approximately 36 miles north of exit 212 on I-90. **GPS:** Recreation Area: 44.345286°, -100.274188°; State Marker: 44.348789°, -100.273215°.

Hours: Open daily May 1 through September 30, 6:00 a.m. to 11:00 p.m.; closes at 9:00 p.m. in off-season.

Admission: Fee charged

Amenities: Historical markers, campground, cabins, showers, RV dump station, hiking, swimming, fishing, and boating; canoe, paddleboat and bicycle rentals are available.

Phone: (605) 773-2885

Email: farmisland@state.sd.us

Fort Sully No. 2

ONIDA, SULLY COUNTY

The U.S. Army built the second Fort Sully in 1866 on a bend of the Missouri about 30 miles north of the old fort. The site was finely situated for steamboat landings, with good views both upstream and down, and amply supplied with timber and grass. In the years to come, the post expanded substantially with many calling it the most attractive of the Missouri River forts. It saw few hostilities in its thirty-year history, most of which was spent as a supply post.

100. Spared from the inundation of Lake Oahe, the marker for the second Fort Sully was moved to the Sully County Courthouse in Oneida.

Fort Sully was abandoned in 1894 and its buildings removed, but local citizens still used the site as a park. They placed a small granite historical marker there in 1929, later removing it to the county courthouse when the river was dammed and the site covered by Lake Oahe.

Location: The marker is in the front lawn of the Sully County Courthouse, 700 Ash Street, Onida SD 57564. GPS: 44.708109°, -100.066142°.

Fort Thompson   ★

FORT THOMPSON, BUFFALO COUNTY

Erected in 1863 as the "Post at Crow Creek Agency," Fort Thompson was the first military post north of Fort Randall established during the Civil War. It was created for the Mdewakanton Dakota forced out of Minnesota after the Dakota Uprising, but hundreds of their people died here from starvation, disease, and other hardships in the transition from woodlands to the dry, exposed plains. Located on the east bank of the Missouri River, the fort included a stockade of about a dozen buildings, which were turned over to the Crow Creek Agency in 1871 and torn down in 1878. The site itself—2 miles south of the town of Fort Thompson—was lost under the river when it was dammed. Fort Thompson is referenced today on the Spirit of the Circle monument stone, placed in memory of the Dakota who lost their lives at the fort.

Location: The monument is on Highway 47 on the Big Bend Dam, just after passing through the Fort Thompson Recreation Area and crossing the spillway. Watch for the circle of flagpoles. GPS: 44.059904°, -99.455865°.

Gordon Stockade

CUSTER, CUSTER COUNTY

John Gordon from Sioux City led a group of twenty-eight gold prospectors illegally into the Black Hills in December 1874 by following the trail left months earlier by the Custer Expedition. After arriving near the site of Custer's permanent camp, they built a stockade with seven cabins for protection from the Lakota and the winter while they panned for gold. Two months of mining brought little gold but plenty of cold, and six of the party abandoned the stockade; the cavalry captured the men and forced them to reveal the camp's location. Troopers took the whole party to Fort Laramie and released them, but some returned to prospect again.

Replicas of the stockade and its cabins were first constructed in 1925, and today's stockade is the third log fortress on the site.

Location: 3.5 miles east of Custer SD, before Custer State Park's west entrance on U.S. Highway 16. **GPS:** 43.769813°, -103.530786°.

Hours: Gordon's Stockade is open year-round, but Custer State Park staff members are on hand for interpretation June through August, 1:00 to 4:00 p.m. daily.

101. The reconstruction of Gordon Stockade in the Black Hills.

Yankton Stockade ★

YANKTON, YANKTON COUNTY

Fear of the Dakota's uprising in Minnesota spreading to the Dakota Territory caused the citizens of the territorial capital of Yankton—joined by refugees from Sioux Falls—to hurriedly build walls for their own defense. A quarter of each block surrounding Third Avenue and Broadway was used to create a square stockade, with each wall about 450 feet long and blockhouses at the northeast and southeast corners. About three hundred lived within the earth-and-timber walls for several weeks, but some fled for Sioux City, including the territorial governor and other officials appointed by President Lincoln. The Indians never attacked and the officials returned to a rather cool reception.

The local DAR chapter placed a boulder marker in 1917 near the center of the stockade but additional street plaques were erected in 1960 to mark the west, north, and east walls of the defense.

102. The DAR marker to the Yankton Stockade.

Locations:

North Wall: West 4th Street between Broadway and Cedar Street. GPS: 42.871068°, -97.396044°.

East Wall: Cedar Street between West 4th and West 3rd. GPS: 42.870495°, -97.395341°.

South Wall and DAR marker: West 3rd and Broadway. GPS: 42.869690°, -97.396717°.

West Wall: West 3rd and Linn Streets. GPS: 42.869800°, -97.398713°.

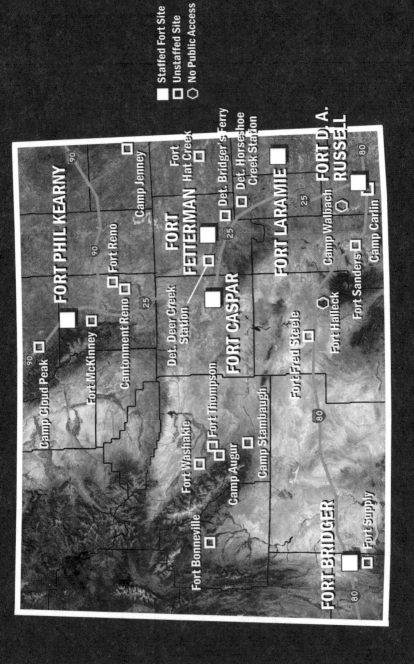

Staffed Fort Site
Unstaffed Site
No Public Access

FORT PHIL KEARNY

Camp Cloud Peak

Fort McKinney

Fort Reno

Cantonment Reno

Camp Jenney

FORT FETTERMAN

Fort Hat Creek

Det. Bridger's Ferry

Det. Horseshoe Creek Station

Det. Deer Creek Station

FORT CASPAR

Fort Thompson

Fort Washakie

Camp Augur

Camp Stambaugh

Fort Bonneville

FORT BRIDGER

Fort Supply

Fort Fred Steele

Fort Halleck

FORT LARAMIE

Camp Walbach

Fort Sanders

FORT D. A. RUSSELL

Camp Carlin

8. Forts of Wyoming

FORTS OF WYOMING

More of a mountain state than a plains state, Wyoming and its forts none-theless figure into the wars for the Northern Plains. The region was home to Shoshone, Cheyenne, Arapahoe, and Lakota, and with trading posts such as Fort Laramie and Fort Bridger, American immigrants on the Oregon, California, and Mormon trails enjoyed a relatively peaceful coexistence with the original inhabitants.

The expansion of western settlement, the discovery of gold in Montana, and the construction of the transcontinental railroad brought conflict. The Shoshone allied with the U.S. government against their longtime enemies, but most of the other tribes fought aggressively to retain control of their land and culture. Posts such as Fort Phil Kearny on the Bozeman Trail and Fort D. A. Russell on the Union Pacific Railroad route challenged the tribes while ensuring people and goods got through, although Fort Phil Kearny ultimately closed due to the resistance.

The forts of the Indian Wars are well-represented in present-day Wyoming, starting with the National Park Service's Fort Laramie National Historic Site. The state of Wyoming also maintains several fort sites as historic attractions, including Forts Phil Kearny, Fred Steele, Bridger, and Fetterman. The city of Casper presents its own Fort Caspar and elements of Fort D. A. Russell survive at F. E. Warren Air Force Base. Many other posts are remembered in buildings and historical markers at or near the original sites.

Camp Brown

Troops from Fort Bridger established the sub-post of Camp Augur in 1869 to protect the Shoshone and miners in the Sweetwater mining district. Originally named for the commander of the Department of the Platte, it was renamed Camp Brown in 1870 for Capt. Frederick H. Brown, killed at the Fetterman Fight; eight years later, the garrison moved to the Little Wind River Reservation where it became Fort Washakie. The original camp site is marked in the city of Lander with a small stone marker downtown embedded in a wall and referencing both camp names but as "forts."

Location: 427 Main Street, Lander WY. GPS: 42.833603°, -108.733831°.

Camp Carlin ★

CHEYENNE, LARAMIE COUNTY

The U.S. Army established a quartermaster depot here in August 1867 for its western campaigns. Officially Cheyenne Depot, it was widely known (and misspelled) as Camp Carlin for its commander, Bvt. Lt. Col. Elias B. Carling. It soon became the second largest quartermaster depot in the United States with sixteen warehouses, more than a thousand civilian employees, and around a hundred military personnel. It supplied a dozen military posts between Fort Omaha in Nebraska and Fort Hall in Idaho for the balance of the Indian wars until closed in 1890. All signs of the camp are now gone, but two historical markers commemorate the post—a six-foot granite marker south of Fort D. A. Russell on Happy Jack Road and a modern metal marker near the fort's east gate on Randall Avenue in Cheyenne. Both provide a brief history of Camp Carlin.

Location: The granite marker is near the address equivalent of 4038 Happy Jack Road, Cheyenne WY, a quarter-mile west of Missile Drive (Warren Air Force Base, Gate 2). The metal marker is on a triangular island at the intersection of Randall and McComb Avenues. GPS: Happy Jack Road Marker: 41.136685°, -104.847839°; Randall Avenue Marker: 41.145313°, -104.836533°.

103. The granite marker to Camp Carlin, south of Warren Air Force Base.

Camp Cloud Peak ★

SHERIDAN, SHERIDAN COUNTY

Gen. George Crook's column encamped in June 1876 at the confluence of the Big and Little Goose Creeks, joined later by Crow and Shoshone allies for war against the Lakota. On June 17 the Lakota defeated Crook on Rosebud Creek in Montana and Crook returned to the campsite—called Camp Cloud Peak—to await reinforcements.

Markers in two parks in Sheridan commemorate this massive encampment of a thousand men and two thousand horses and mules. In Kendrick Park, the local DAR chapter placed a boulder with a plaque to mark the site in 1939; in Mill Park is the 1938 "Crook's Fountain," built of natural stone with interpretive signage nearby.

Location: The boulder is to the north of the park's concession stand (address equivalent is 2 Badger Street, Sheridan WY). The fountain is at the intersection of West Dow Street and North Jefferson (West Ager) in Sheridan. GPS: Boulder: 44.799905°, -106.964747°; Fountain: 44.802771°, -106.958876°.

Camp Jenney

NEWCASTLE, WESTON COUNTY

An 1857 expedition led by Lt. G. K. Warren to survey the Black Hills was the first military encampment made at the site now called Camp Jenney, later named for Professor Walter P. Jenney and his military escort who camped here in 1875; gold seekers again used the site that winter. A 1940 stone marker and a newer state marker commemorate Camp Jenney and the Jenney Stockade near the site, and an original cabin from the stockade and stage station on the Deadwood Trail survives in Newcastle.

Location: Historical markers are located on U.S. Highway 16, on a pull-off 3 miles east of U.S. Highway 85. The cabin is at the **Anna Miller Museum**, 401 Delaware Avenue, Newcastle WY 82701. GPS: Marker: 43.816064°, -104.122990°; Cabin: 43.850597°, -104.193338°.

104. An original cabin from the Camp Jenney site is now at the Anna Miller Museum in Newcastle.

Cantonment Reno   ★

KAYCEE, JOHNSON COUNTY

Troopers built Cantonment Reno in 1876 at the Bozeman Trail's crossing of the Powder River to guard a temporary supply post and escort supply trains through the area. Most Indians were on reservations by 1878, so the post was moved outside of Buffalo, Wyoming, and renamed Fort McKinney. Small modern plaques offer interpretation of the post near the original site.

Location: About 23 miles east of Kaycee, WY. Travel east for about 18 miles on paved Highway 1002; before the highway makes the sharp bend south, turn north on the gravel Lower Sussex Road, traveling nearly 5 miles to the plaques. (Be advised that the Fort Reno site [page 218] is just 4 miles further north.) GPS: 43.782226°, -106.268102°.

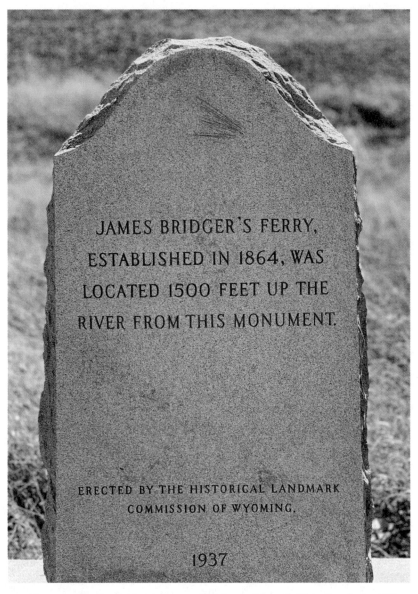

JAMES BRIDGER'S FERRY,
ESTABLISHED IN 1864, WAS
LOCATED 1500 FEET UP THE
RIVER FROM THIS MONUMENT.

ERECTED BY THE HISTORICAL LANDMARK
COMMISSION OF WYOMING.

1937

105. Monument to Jim Bridger's Ferry, which hosted the 11th Ohio Cavalry in 1886.

Detachment at Bridger's Ferry ★

ORIN, CONVERSE COUNTY

Jim Bridger established a ferry in 1864 to serve traffic crossing the North Platte River. In 1866, "galvanized Yankees" of the 11th Ohio Cavalry were assigned to guard the ferry, employing howitzer cannons at each landing. The military prevented raids on the ferry and protected supplies heading to posts farther north. The Historical Landmark Commission of Wyoming placed a granite marker near the site in 1937 to commemorate the ferry.

Location: The marker is 2 miles east of the I-25 exit for Orin on Highway 319, on a pull-off just south of the North Platte River bridge. GPS: 42.648480°, -105.163744°.

Detachment at Deer Creek Station ★

GLENROCK, CONVERSE COUNTY

Deer Creek Station on the North Platte River was familiar to Oregon, California, and Mormon Trail travelers in the late 1850s and 1860s, especially those needing supplies, repairs, and refreshment. It served the Pony Express while it was active in from 1860 to 1861, but hostilities with native peoples compelled the army to establish a detachment across the road from Deer Creek Station in 1862. The increased fighting forced the station's owner to abandon it in 1864, and Indians burned the site in 1866.

Location: An historical marker to the station is on the southeast corner of South Fourth and Cedar Streets in Glenrock, south of the downtown area at the town park. GPS: 42.860129°, -105.871816°.

530 YARDS SOUTH EAST OF
THIS MONUMENT ON THE
OREGON TRAIL WAS THE SITE OF
HORSESHOE CREEK PONY EXPRESS
AND U. S. MILITARY TELEGRAPH
AND STAGE STATION BUILT IN 1860.

ERECTED BY THE HISTORICAL LANDMARK
COMMISSION OF WYOMING.

1937

106. Horseshoe Creek Station marker.

Detachment at Horseshoe Creek Station ★

GLENDO, PLATTE COUNTY

Originally a mail and passenger station built by the Mormons in 1856, Horseshoe Creek Station also served as a Pony Express station from 1860 to 1861. A detachment of a lieutenant and thirty-eight men were stationed here in 1862 to guard travelers and the telegraph line, and in 1866 it was a stop on John "Portugee" Phillips's legendary ride from Fort Phil Kearny to Fort Laramie (page 208). A state historical marker commemorates the station, as does an adjacent granite marker for the Pony Express.

Location: The markers are 2 miles south of Glendo on the South Glendo Highway (Highway 319) at a pull-off. **GPS:** 42.471532°, -105.027757°.

Fort Bonneville ★

DANIEL, SUBLETTE COUNTY

The reason for this fortress isn't entirely clear. Originating out of Fort Osage, Missouri, in 1832 Capt. Benjamin Bonneville and his expedition of 110 men built the stockaded fort along the Green River in the heart of trapping territory. Most think the fort was to promote the Rocky Mountain fur trade,

107. The DAR's 1915 boulder to the questionably purposed Fort Bonneville.

but some historians believe Fort Bonneville was a front for the U.S. Army's reconnaissance efforts in the area. In any event, Bonneville constructed the fort late in the fall and heavy snows drove them out that winter. The DAR marked the site with a granite boulder in 1915, and a state historical marker is also located at the site.

Location: The markers are found on Highway 354, northwest of Daniel; travel 1.75 miles north of town on U.S. Highway 189, make a left on U.S. Highway 191 for a quarter-mile, and proceed a little more than 3 miles on Highway 354 to the site. GPS: 42.892967°, -110.136363°.

Fort Bridger

FORT BRIDGER, UINTA COUNTY

Famed frontiersman Jim Bridger built his small fort and blacksmith shop in 1843 on Groshon Creek as an emigrant supply stop on the Oregon Trail. Mormons apparently forced Bridger out of the fort in 1853, although they claimed to have bought it; in any event, he returned to reclaim his fort in 1857, backed by federal troops who marched on to Salt Lake City in the so-called Mormon War. The Mormons destroyed the fort rather than surrender it.

108. The log-and-frame officer's quarters was among the first structures built at Fort Bridger in 1858.

Bridger leased the site to the U.S. Army as a supply depot in 1858, and troops began erecting log structures around a parade ground, ultimately building it into a permanent military post. For the next thirty years, Fort Bridger was a base for troops protecting emigrants and Union Pacific work crews as well as a supply point for geological expeditions, surveyors, miners, lumbermen, and ranchers.

By 1890, however, traffic and threats along the trails dwindled to the point where the army abandoned Fort Bridger. William A. Carter—the post sutler since the 1850s—expanded his operations and ownership of the old fort's military reservation, eventually becoming one of the largest cattle producers in Wyoming. He sold some of the fort's buildings and preserved others during the development of the town of Fort Bridger.

The fort became a Wyoming Historical Landmark in 1933 when the Carter family donated the grounds and buildings to the state. More original land and buildings were bought and restored, and today's **Fort Bridger State Historic Site** covers thirty-seven acres with twenty-seven historic structures. Costumed staff and volunteers provide interpretation for the state site, which now includes the restored sutler's complex, buildings from the military period, and the old barracks and milk barn, which serves as the site's museum.

109. The post commissary (*left*) and old guardhouse were built in 1867 and 1868, respectively, both of limestone quarried 2 miles west of Fort Bridger.

Every Labor Day weekend, Fort Bridger hosts an annual Mountain Man Rendezvous to celebrate the "Jim Bridger" era of the fort. Attendees can enjoy native dancing, black-powder competitions, traditional music, foods from the 1800s, and other vendors, entertainment, and activities.

Location: Fort Bridger State Historic Site, 37000 I-80BL, Fort Bridger WY 82933. Approximately 30 miles east of Evanston, WY via I-80; take exit 34 from I-80 and drive 2.5 miles southeast to the park entrance. **GPS:** 41.317966°, -110.390104°.

Hours: Buildings open daily, May through September, 9:00 a.m. to 5:00 p.m.; grounds open year-round.

Admission: Fee charged

Amenities: Original and replica historic buildings, visitor center, museum, gift shop, restrooms, picnic area, and interpretive trail.

Phone: (307) 782-3842

Website: https://wyoparks.wyo.gov/index.php/places-to-go/fort-bridger

Fort Caspar

CASPER, NATRONA COUNTY

Native people long frequented this bend of the North Platte River where Mormon emigrants established a ferry in 1847. A toll bridge followed in 1853, followed by a second bridge and trading post, known as Platte Bridge Station, in 1859. The station was the first permanent settlement in what became Casper, and virtually everyone and everything came through here including the Mormon Trail, the Oregon and California Trails, the Overland Stage, the Pony Express, and the transcontinental telegraph line.

U.S. troops built a small fort at the site in 1855 and stationed here during the "Mormon War" of 1858–59. In 1862 another company of troops came to the Platte Bridge Station to protect telegraph lines in the area. Hostilities peaked in 1865 when almost three thousand Lakota, Cheyenne, and Arapahoe from the Powder River country gathered to attack the station. On July 26 they ambushed a small detachment led by Lt. Caspar Collins escorting an army supply train. The troops fought their way back to the station, but Collins and four men were killed in what was known as the Battle of the Platte Bridge. The supply train was also attacked, and only three of the twenty-five men survived the Battle of Red Buttes.

The Army renamed the station Fort Casper for the fallen officer (unintentionally misspelling his first name) and enlarged and rebuilt it in 1866. The fort closed in 1867, however, after Fort Fetterman opened, with troops taking as many building materials as they could to the new post. In 1936, citizens of Casper—also spelled incorrectly—took action to restore the fort's legacy. They rebuilt Fort Caspar as a WPA project, reconstructing many of its buildings at their original locations. Its name was spelled correctly this time around.

The reconstructions and exhibits are part of the **Fort Caspar Museum and Historic Site** complex, owned and operated by the City of Casper. The museum opened in 1983 and includes exhibits from the social and natural history of central Wyoming, from prehistoric occupation through recent times. The reconstruction consists of a sutler's store, officers' quarters, stables, blacksmith shop, commissary, mess hall, barracks, and telegraph office with each of the buildings furnished as they were in 1865.

Location: Fort Caspar Museum, 4001 Fort Caspar Road, Casper, WY 82604. **GPS:** 42.836089°, -106.370695°.

Hours: Open daily May through September, 8:00 a.m. to 5:00 p.m.; winter hours are the same, although closed Mondays and Sundays and fort buildings are locked.

110. The reconstructed Fort Caspar is part of a museum and historic site complex, owned by the city of Casper.

Admission: Fee charged

Amenities: Reconstructed buildings, historical markers, tours, museum, gift shop and bookstore, special events (check website), picnic area and restrooms.

Phone: (307) 235-8462

Email: ryoung@casperwy.gov

Website: fortcasparwyoming.com

Fort D. A. Russell

F. E. WARREN AIR FORCE BASE, CHEYENNE, LARAMIE COUNTY

Now part of a U.S. Air Force without a runway, Fort D. A. Russell began its existence very much focused on transportation.

The fort and adjacent town of Cheyenne were both founded on July 4, 1867, to protect and supply the transcontinental Union Pacific Railroad as rail crews made their way west toward the Rockies. The fort (named for Civil War general David A. Russell) became an important supply point for the military due to its location between the country's borders and the coasts. Tents and log cabins went up first, followed by wood frame buildings as the expanse of the fort increased.

After it became a permanent army post in 1884, the War Department ordered Fort D. A. Russell rebuilt to serve eight infantry companies with twenty-seven brick buildings. It was the only active fort in Wyoming by the time of the Spanish-American War in 1898, and the troops mobilized there were the first to reach the walls of Manila in the Philippines and raise the American flag.

The army put in a flying field in 1919, mostly for a cross-country mail route. After sixty years at Fort D. A. Russell, the last cavalry units left the post in 1927 and the last horse left in 1943. It was renamed Fort F. E. Warren in 1930 after Senator Francis E. Warren, a Civil War Medal of Honor recipient, past mayor of Cheyenne, and the last territorial and first state governor of Wyoming. The fort became an army air base in 1947 and was renamed as F. E. Warren Air Force Base in 1949.

As mentioned, Warren is an Air Force base without a runway or a single fixed-wing aircraft; what makes it an airbase is about 150 Minuteman III missiles and hosting the 90th Missile Wing of the Air Force Global Strike Command.

A staggering amount of architectural history survives at Warren—214 historic homes are among the more than eight hundred buildings at the base. Almost all of the buildings are used by the Air Force today, including the homes of Gen. John "Black Jack" Pershing and Gen. Billy Mitchell, "Father of the U.S. Air Force." (Pershing never occupied the house, but it was available to his wife when he was on campaign.)

The **Warren Intercontinental Ballistic Missile (ICBM) and Heritage Museum** covers the history of the installation from its 1867 founding as a cavalry post through its present-day status as the most powerful missile wing in the free world. The museum is open to the general public, but non-military members wanting to visit must contact the museum for availability and access and provide full name, birth date, and driver's license number at least three business days (seventy-two hours) before arrival at Warren AFB.

Location: Warren ICBM and Heritage Museum, 401 Champagne Drive Building 31, F.E. Warren AFB WY 82005. Warren Air Force Base is northwest of the junction of I-25 and I-80 at Cheyenne. **GPS:** 41.156246°, -104.864179°.

Hours: Monday through Friday, 9:00 a.m. to 4:00 p.m.; closed federal holidays.

Admission: Free

Phone: (307) 773-2980

Website: warrenmuseum.com

Fort Fetterman ★★★

DOUGLAS, CONVERSE COUNTY

Because the Bozeman Trail forts of Reno, Phil Kearny, and C. F. Smith were under continual siege, an intermediate fort was built between them and Fort Laramie to quell the attacks. Named for Capt. William J. Fetterman of Fort Phil Kearny massacre fame, **Fort Fetterman** was built on a plateau above the North Platte River. The location was a horrible mistake, as violent and almost constant winds ripped at the tents of troops throughout the winter of 1867–68.

The men dug in, however, and built a solid little post that helped keep the Bozeman open until the Treaty of 1868 closed the trail and its forts. Fort Fetterman then stood alone on a desolate frontier where comforts were hard to find. No towns were nearby and female companionship was missing for the

111. The former officers' quarters serve today as Fort Fetterman State Historic Site's visitor center.

enlisted men (with the exception of the banned "Hog Ranch" brothel across the river). Fresh fruit and vegetables weren't available and gardens quickly died in the hot dry winds. Entertainment was rare and desertion was common, since most saw service at Fort Fetterman as an undeserved punishment.

The little fort played a big role in the Plains Indian Wars during the 1870s, however, serving as a supply base, headquarters, and marshalling point for expeditions into the Powder River country. General Crook used Fort Fetterman as a base for his three expeditions in 1876, culminating in the Battle of Powder River, the Battle of the Rosebud, and the defeat of Dull Knife near the Powder River.

This last battle, combined with others in 1876 and 1877, ended the major phase of the Northern Plains war and the need for Fort Fetterman. It was abandoned in 1882, with most of the buildings moved or stripped to supply the surrounding timber-starved "Fetterman City." This rip-roaring frontier town disappeared when the town of Douglas came into prominence, and the remaining fort structures were sold, dismantled, or moved to other locations. When the state took over the site in 1961, only the vandalized log-and-adobe officers' quarters and ordnance storehouse remained.

The fort was a hardship post in its time, and it's not difficult to imagine that today at the **Fort Fetterman State Historic Site**. There are no shade trees, the surrounding hills of brown and yellowing grasses go on for miles and miles, and the wind never seems to end.

The two restored buildings of the fort include the officers' quarters—now its visitor center—and the ordnance storehouse, which includes maps, drawings, photographs and artifacts from the fort. Interpretive signs describe former buildings and activities, with corners of the original buildings marked. An interpretive trail passes through the historic site and leads to a gazebo overlooking Crook's Camp and the Indian Country to the north. You'll pass a Bozeman Trail marker indicating its route and can view ruts remaining from the 1860s.

Location: Fort Fetterman State Historic Site, 752 Highway 93, Douglas, WY 82633. From I-25, take exit 140 at Douglas and travel 7 miles on Highway 93. **GPS:** 42.842995, -105.485783°.

Hours: Open from Memorial Day through Labor Day, Tuesday through Saturday, 9:00 a.m. to 5:00 p.m.; closed September through May.

Admission: Fee charged

Amenities: Visitor center, historical features, overlooks, self-guided tour, gift shop, and hiking.

Phone: (307) 358-9288

Fort Fred Steele ★★

RAWLINS, CARBON COUNTY

Built in 1868, Fort Fred Steele was the last of three military forts (with D. A. Russell and Sanders) built in Wyoming to protect Union Pacific work crews. Named for Col. Frederick Steele, a commander at the Battle of Vicksburg, the fort supplied military expeditions and provided the force behind law and order during early Wyoming territorial days.

The Army ordered the fort abandoned in 1886, at which point the town of Fort Steele began. The town eked out an existence as a Union Pacific stop and later as a Lincoln Highway fueling and rest stop, but after the rerouting of both the rail and highway Fort Steele withered away.

Both Fort Steeles are commemorated at the appropriately desolate **Fort Fred Steele Historic Site**. Little grows here in the arid climate and most

112. Ruins of barracks at Fort Fred Steele. Many of the structures were converted to civilian purposes in the town of Fort Steele after the fort was closed, so this site may have been a hotel.

buildings are long gone, but it's still fascinating to walk the grounds for the interpretive markers that tell the stories that the remains cannot.

Location: Fort Fred Steele State Historic Site is 13 miles east of Rawlins off I-80, exit 228, 1.25 miles north of rest area. **GPS:** 41.777853°, -106.946089°.

Admission: Free

Amenities: Historic structures and ruins, historical and interpretive markers, restrooms, water (at rest stop), fishing, and river access.

Fort Hat Creek   ★★

LUSK, NIOBRARA COUNTY

Capt. James Egan established a stockaded sub-post of Fort Laramie on Sage Creek next to the Hat Creek stage station in 1875 to help keep miners out of the Black Hills. Since it was on Sage Creek, it was sometimes referred to as Camp at Sage Creek but also as Fort Hat Creek, perpetuating the mistaken name of the stage station; no matter the name, they abandoned it the next year. The stage station burned in 1883 and was replaced by a log structure

113. DAR monument to the Old Fort Hat Creek and its stage station.

which still stands today. In 1927, the local DAR chapter placed a stone monument and plaque to Old Fort Hat Creek at the site.

Location: From U.S. Highway 18 (12 miles north of Lusk), take Hat Creek Road east for 2 miles to Stage Road and then south for 1 mile to the site. The postal address is the equivalent of 860 Stage Road, Lusk WY. **GPS:** 42.930504°, -104.342904°.

Fort Laramie

FT. LARAMIE, GOSHEN COUNTY

William Sublette established his fur trading post in 1834 at the North Platte and Laramie Rivers confluence, selling the log-stockade fort the next year to Jim Bridger, who in turn sold it in 1836 to the American Fur Company. The new owners vastly improved the property which regular traders came to call Fort Laramie.

Fur trade declined in the 1840s while wagon traffic increased. Thousands of emigrants from the Oregon and Mormon Trails stopped at the fort, trading with Indians, buying supplies, and making repairs to their wagons and clothing. The time was right in 1849 for the U.S. government to become the fourth owner of the fort, as the War Department wanted posts along the Oregon Trail to protect the traffic.

That year's California gold rush brought thousands more through the new military post. Troops cut and sawed timber for new structures in addition to the original adobe fort, including the two-story officer's quarters (later known as "Old Bedlam"), a block of soldiers' quarters, a bakery, and two stables.

Antagonism between natives and non-natives grew, leading to an 1851 treaty council that brought more than ten thousand Lakota, Cheyenne, Arapahoe, Snake, and Crow tribe members to the fort. The council moved down the North Platte to Horse Creek to find grass for the ponies, and the resulting Horse Creek Treaty brought peace for all of three years until the nearby Grattan Fight enflamed the plains for thirty-five years to come.

The military planned to abandon Fort Laramie in 1857 but ended up using it as a supply base against the Cheyenne and reportedly rebellious Mormons in Utah. The fort continued to grow from increased freighting, sustained emigration, discovery of gold in Colorado, and establishment of telegraph lines. At the end of the Civil War, Fort Laramie staged the final assaults on

114. Fort Laramie National Historic Site on the Laramie River.

115. 1874 cavalry barracks.

Northern Plains Indians and hosted the 1868 Fort Laramie Treaty, which gave the Lakota control of the sacred Black Hills.

The U.S. Army ordered Fort Laramie abandoned in 1890. Land and buildings changed hands over the years while tenants, absentee landowners, and souvenir hunters stripped the buildings. Local people erected a monument to both the fort and Oregon Trail in 1913, and later created a commission for the public ownership and preservation of Fort Laramie. The state of Wyoming bought the surviving buildings and 214 acres for donation to the U.S. government, which in 1938 created the Fort Laramie National Monument.

Fort Laramie National Historic Site, as it is known today, is one of the better-preserved frontier military posts, having saved and restored nearly a dozen buildings to their original appearance. Nine standing ruins are preserved to fill the grounds and contribute to the rich history of the post.

The best-known and oldest building on the grounds is "Old Bedlam," the former bachelor officers' quarters. Built in 1849, Old Bedlam's right-side interior has been restored to the 1850s era and the left to the 1863–64 period. The building was the center of social life at Fort Laramie, as one might imagine with young unmarried officers as the occupants.

Before touring the grounds and the buildings (and budget about two hours for doing so), stop at the former commissary, today's visitor center.

116. "Old Bedlam" bachelor officers' quarters.

Here you can view a variety of exhibits relating to the history of Fort Laramie and western expansion to set the stage for your visit. A film on the post's history is available, as are ranger-guided tours, talks, and demonstrations during the summer.

Location: Fort Laramie National Historic Site, 965 Gray Rocks Road, Fort Laramie, WY 82212. At the town of Fort Laramie, turn south on State Route 160, and drive 3 miles to the park entrance. **GPS:** 42.202176°, -104.558213°.

Hours: Fort grounds are open daily from dawn until dusk. The fort museum and visitor center open daily at 8:00 a.m. with extended hours during the summer; closed Thanksgiving, Christmas, and New Year's Day.

Admission: Free

Amenities: Historical buildings and markers, living history displays, tours, restrooms, gift shop, and bookstore. The Fort Laramie Historical Association Bookstore at the visitor center is one of the finest western history bookstores in the region and sells more than 650 titles on western history topics.

Phone: (307) 837-2221

Website: nps.gov/fola/

Note: The monument for the **Grattan Fight** (also called the Grattan Massacre)—the event which started the Great Sioux War—is nearby. Take U.S. Highway 26 southeast for 5 miles to Highway 157; drive south for 2 miles and east for 2 miles to get to the stone marker on the north side of the road.

Fort McKinney ★★

BUFFALO, JOHNSON COUNTY

Fort McKinney began as Cantonment Reno (above), which was renamed McKinney Depot in 1877 to honor Lt. John A. McKinney, killed the year before in a fight at the Red Fork of the Powder River. The War Department moved the post fifty miles north to the Bighorn foothills in 1878, whereupon Gen. Philip H. Sheridan recommended it for fort status.

Fort McKinney started with cheap, rough buildings, but the post received an upgrade in the 1880s. It suffered from huge distances to rail and river and saw little service during the Indian Wars, however, and it was abandoned in 1894 with the buildings and land given to the state of Wyoming. The fort got a new life in 1903 when the state moved the Wyoming Soldiers' and Sailors' Home from Cheyenne to Fort McKinney. A few buildings from the fort are still there, the most visible of which is the former post hospital. There are no displays at the site, but a historical marker is on U.S. Highway 16 and visitors are welcome on the grounds.

Location: Veterans' Home of Wyoming, 700 Veterans Lane, Buffalo, WY 82834 (2 miles west of Buffalo on U.S. Highway 16). **GPS**: 44.332998°, -106.739255°.

Phone: (307) 684-9331

117. Fort McKinney's 1880 hospital.

The **Jim Gatchell Memorial Museum** in nearby Buffalo is one of the top museums of the Old West and provides considerable history on the region's role in the wars. As owner of the first drugstore in Johnson County, Jim Gatchell met and befriended cowboys, Indians, lawmen, settlers, cattle barons, and famous army scouts, many of whom gifted him remarkable mementos and artifacts, all of which he agreed to donate to the county provided a museum was built to house them. The museum was named as a winner of the 2023 National Medal for Museum and Library Service in ceremonies at the White House.

Location: 100 Fort Street, Buffalo, WY 82834. **GPS:** 44.348056°, -106.699796°.

Hours: Memorial Day through Labor Day, Monday through Saturday, 9:00 a.m. to 5:00 p.m., Sunday, noon to 5:00 p.m.; winter hours: Monday through Friday, 9:00 a.m. to 4:00 p.m.

Admission: Fee charged

Phone: (307) 684-9331

Email: educator@jimgatchell.com

Website: www.jimgatchell.com

Fort Phil Kearny ★★★★

BANNER, SHERIDAN COUNTY

Fort Phil Kearny—along with Forts Reno and C. F. Smith—was built in 1866 to protect traffic along the Bozeman Trail between Fort Laramie and the gold fields of Montana. As the forts pressed against the Lakota and Cheyenne prime hunting lands, however, violence was guaranteed.

Col. Henry B. Carrington and the 18th Infantry selected the site on the Piney Fork of the Powder River. Using timber from the surrounding foothills of the Bighorn Mountains, Carrington built a substantial stockade fort of eleven acres with civilians adding a seven-acre corral to create one of the largest and best-fortified forts of the frontier. Its construction, however, brought continuous harassment and attacks by Oglala warriors of Red Cloud, along with Northern Cheyenne and Arapaho tribes. The fort's first six months of existence saw more than 50 hostile demonstrations, the killing of 154 white men, and the theft of 800 head of livestock. Emigrants were regularly attacked, equipment was continually stolen or destroyed, and even heavily guarded supply trains had to run a gauntlet to get to and from the fort.

118. Aerial view of the Fort Phil Kearny State Historic Site's walking paths denote the original walls of the stockaded post.

The most devastating attack came on December 21, 1866, when eighty infantry and cavalry troops led by Capt. William J. Fetterman chased a small war party, only to be wiped out once beyond the view of the fort by hundreds of Lakota, Cheyenne, and Arapaho warriors. Carrington hired riders to carry word of the disaster, one of whom was John "Portugee" Phillips. Phillips completed the 236-mile ride to Fort Laramie through a freezing snowstorm and enemy territory in only three days, an amazing feat that made him an instant legend.

Carrington was replaced in January 1867 in accordance with orders received prior to the Fetterman fight. Harassment of the fort and trail continued throughout the year, but troops did claim a victory in August of that year. Using newly issued breech-loading Springfield rifles, they successfully defended a group of woodcutters from a far larger Lakota force in the Wagon Box Fight.

The following year brought no relief for the trail and the forts along it. Exasperated in its inability to defend against or control the Indians, the government gave up the region in return for other concessions, and Fort Phil Kearny and the other posts along the Bozeman were ordered closed.

119. A reconstructed portion of Fort Phil Kearny's stockade.

The last soldiers left the fort in August 1868 and the Indians soon burned it to the ground.

When the site of Fort Phil Kearny became a national historic landmark in 1960, the surrounding area was little changed in nearly a hundred years. Today, on the plateau under the shadows of the Bighorn Mountains, you can stand at **Fort Phil Kearny State Historic Site** and easily imagine Captain Fetterman headed over the Lodge Trail Ridge toward disaster, or "Portugee" Phillips headed south for Fort Laramie on horseback in a snowstorm.

120. Fetterman Massacre monument.

Start your visit at the visitor center and museum, which includes information on the fort and conflict, along with dioramas and artifacts. The grounds of the fort include a partial stockade reconstruction, with portions of it at each corner of the fort. Markers surrounding the parade ground and its all-weather gravel walk describe the buildings that formerly occupied the site, and a display with a recording further enhances the walk. Plan for at least one to two hours at the site.

Location: Fort Phil Kearny State Historic Site, 528 Wagon Box Road, Banner, WY 82832. The site is 20 miles south of Sheridan or 18 miles north of Buffalo on I-90 at exit 44. **GPS:** 44.533288°, -106.827258°.

Hours: Visitor center open daily June through September, 8:00 a.m. to 6:00 p.m.; open daily in May from noon to 4:00 p.m.; open Wednesday through Sunday in October from noon to 4:00 p.m.; closed from November through April, but open by appointment.

Admission: Fee charged

Amenities: Visitor center, museum, interpretive signage, book and gift shop, living history programs and events, trails, restrooms, water, and picnic tables. Tours are available upon request and by appointment by contacting the fort site.

Phone: (307) 684-7629

Email: sharie.shada@wyo.gov

Website: fortphilkearny.com

Related History: The **Portugee Phillip's Ride** memorial is 300 yards down the hill from Fort Phil Kearny. The site of the **Fetterman Fight** (also called the Fetterman Massacre or the Fetterman Disaster) is less than 2 miles to the north at the end of a now closed-off U.S. Highway 87 and features the 1908 stone marker and a self-guided walking tour. The **Wagon Box Fight** site is a left (west) turn from the Fort Phil Kearny entrance and then 4 miles on the mostly gravel Wagon Box Road; the historic site includes a small walk with historic and interpretive markers.

Fort Reno ★

Fort Reno was built in 1865 along with Forts Phil Kearny and C. F. Smith to protect the Bozeman Trail. Brig. Gen. Patrick E. Connor selected the site, and it was originally named Fort Connor but soon renamed for Maj. Jesse L. Reno killed in the Civil War. Although intended to be temporary, the troops nonetheless built up the fort with blockhouses and bastions at two corners of the cottonwood stockade. The men abandoned the fort with the Treaty of 1868 and Indians soon destroyed it. The state and local residents placed a stone marker at the site in 1914.

Location: The Fort Reno site is about 27 miles east of Kaycee on Lower Sussex Road, about 4 miles north of the Cantonment Reno site above. The road turns to gravel about a mile and a half north of the Cantonment site; watch for the stone Fort Reno marker in the field to the right after about another 2.5 miles. **GPS:** 43.827401°, -106.240384°.

Note: Your state map shows you can take this road directly into Buffalo WY. While this route is shorter and follows the historic trail, you'll probably regret it unless you love washboard roads. It's recommended that you double back to Kaycee for the interstate.

Fort Sanders

Fort Sanders—named for Union general William P. Sanders—was built in 1866 to protect the Overland Trail and then work crews of the Union Pacific Railroad as they toiled toward the Rockies. The tracks reached the fort in 1868, the same year former general and then-presidential candidate Ulysses S. Grant visited with other former generals to campaign for soldier and rail worker votes.

Fort Sanders' troops fought in twenty major skirmishes, but once Fort D. A. Russell was completed at Cheyenne late in 1868, the need for Fort Sanders waned. Troops abandoned it in 1882.

Today, U.S. Highway 287 cuts through the site with a historical marker telling the story of Fort Sanders. It also indicates the location of two sets

121. The ruins of the Fort Sanders guardhouse still stand outside of Laramie.

of ruins—the powder house to the northeast and the guardhouse to the northwest.

Location: The marker is at the intersection of U.S. Highway 287 and Cavalryman Ranch Road, a mile south of Laramie. The guardhouse and 1914 DAR marker are a quarter-mile west on Cavalryman Ranch, turn right to South Kiowa Road, and right to the ruins. **GPS:** Marker: 41.268377°, -105.595738°; Guardhouse: 41.271293°, -105.598168°.

Fort Stambaugh ★

ATLANTIC CITY, FREMONT COUNTY

A threat to gold miners in the Sweetwater District brought Fort Stambaugh to the southern edge of the Wind River Range for their protection in 1870. Named for Lt. Charles B. Stambaugh killed in battle earlier that year, the post included four log barracks for two companies of infantry. The decline in mining brought the end and abandonment the fort in 1878. A granite marker placed in 1959 on South Pass Road commemorates the post, 6 miles to the east and unmarked.

Location: The marker is about 2.25 miles north of the village of Atlantic City. From Lander, WY, drive 8.5 miles south on U.S. Highway 287; continue south on Highway 28 for about 17 miles and turn left on South Pass Road for a mile and half to the marker's pull-off. **GPS**: 42.526658°, -108.722977°.

Fort Supply

ROBERTSON, UINTA COUNTY

Mormons built Fort Supply in 1853 as a small supply post 10 miles south of Fort Bridger for Latter-day Saints headed to the Salt Lake Valley. They added a log stockade around it after a few years, but burned the entire site to the ground in 1857 with the approach of U.S. troops during the so-called Mormon War. The Historical Landmark Commission of Wyoming marked the site with a granite slab and plaque in 1937.

Location: To reach the Fort Supply State Historic Site, travel 1 mile south of Robertson on a gravel road, then 2 miles west to the site near Willow Creek. **GPS**: 41.166920°, -110.437697°.

122. Fort Supply State Historic Site.

Fort Thompson ★

LANDER, FREMONT COUNTY

A temporary field camp, this post was built in 1857 by troops from Fort Kearny, Nebraska Territory, while surveying a road to Oregon. According to the state marker at the site, W. M. F. Magraw was the superintendent for the road project, who was later fired for mismanagement by U.S. Secretary of the Interior Jacob Thompson who had authorized the road. Camp Magraw and Fort Thompson are both listed as names for the post, but an adjacent stone marker placed by the local Boy Scout troop identifies it as Fort McGraw.

Location: The markers are about 2 miles northeast of Lander on a Highway 789 pull-off. **GPS:** 42.851731°, -108.696139°.

123. Unique marker created by a local Boy Scout troop for Fort McGraw, an alternate name to Fort Thompson.

Fort Washakie ★★

After the Shoshone received a new agency in 1871 at the Wind River Reservation, troops were transferred from Fort Brown (page 190) to this site. In 1878, the War Department made the unusual but politically advantageous move of renaming the fort for Washakie, the tribe's chief and an ally of the United States. Fort Washakie became a staging point for campaigns against Plains Indians and explorations of the Great Basin and Yellowstone Park.

The fort closed in 1909 and ownership transferred to the Wind River Reservation. The Shoshone tribal government uses many of Fort Washakie's original stone buildings, and though not open to the public, they are easily spotted in the north side of Fort Washakie. The most historic is the Old Block House, built in 1871 by the agency to protect women and children in event of attack. It is south of town, located at the end of an unpaved, unnamed side road south of the Shoshone Roads building at Trout Creek Road and Old

124. 1871 blockhouse built for the protection of women and children of the Wind River Agency.

Wind River Highway. Visitors will also want to see the granite marker to Chief Washakie and pay respects to his grave at the town's cemetery.

Location: The blockhouse is at the address equivalent of 257 Old Wind River Highway, Fort Washakie, WY 82514. Marker is immediately west of Fort Washakie on North Fork Road at the entrance to the cemetery. Washakie's grave is within the stone wall of the cemetery near the southwest corner. **GPS:** Blockhouse: 42.985192°, -108.887546°; Marker: 43.006506°, -108.881843°; Grave: 43.004685°, -108.890896°.

ACKNOWLEDGMENTS

Writing (and sometimes traveling) is a lonely job, but there are always those along the way who help to get the job done.

First, my friends Ron and Judy Parks, who helped realize my dream of this guide appearing in color, and who also supported my excursions around the Northern Plains to sites unseen and waiting to be photographed. They are truly wonderful people who share my love of history and passion for the natural beauty of the land where history takes place. They have my eternal gratitude, along with Leslie Fattig of the Nebraska State Historical Society Foundation, for getting this book to fruition.

It's been more than fifteen years since the first edition of this book came out, and during the interim the acquaintanceships made with the folks at the Nebraska forts have grown into friendships. A special thanks to Jim Domeier and Mary Hughes at Fort Hartsuff State Historical Park, Jason Grof and John Slader at Fort Atkinson State Historical Park, Gene Hunt at Fort Kearny State Historical Park, and Bob Hanover at the Nebraska Game and Parks Commission.

My appreciation to Bridget Barry, editor in chief at the University of Nebraska Press and my editor for the guide's publication with Bison Books. I have always wanted to write for the best-known publisher of my home state, and it was the original intention of us both to travel this trail together back in 2008. Sometimes you have to take a detour but we're back on the main trail.

There are those who enjoy seeing what I do and constantly prop me up during the writing and research process. I can always count on my great friends Paul Horsted, Russell Gifford, John Seals, and Randa Zalman, who seem to share my enthusiasm for this lifestyle. I always feel compelled to write something they'll enjoy. Thank you all.

Finally, love and appreciation to my wife Susan, who has now braved the writing and publishing of my eighth book. This one probably took the greatest patience and understanding as we traveled the seven featured states together for probably twenty thousand miles, her taking the wheel for a few thousand of them. We continue to make our wonderful journey together.

BIBLIOGRAPHY

Barnes, Jeff. *Forts of the Northern Plains.* Mechanicsburg PA: Stackpole Books, 2008.

Carley, Kenneth. *The Dakota War of 1862: Minnesota's Other Civil War.* St. Paul: Minnesota Historical Society Press, 1976.

Dahlin, Curtis A. *A Guidebook to the U.S.-Dakota War of 1862 in Minnesota.* Willmar MN: Lakeside, 2019.

DeLorme. *Iowa Atlas & Gazetteer.* 2nd ed. Yarmouth ME: DeLorme, 2001.

———. *Minnesota Atlas & Gazetteer.* 8th ed. Yarmouth ME: DeLorme, 2013.

———. *Montana Atlas & Gazetteer.* 4th ed. Yarmouth ME: DeLorme, 2001.

———. *Nebraska Atlas & Gazetteer.* 3rd ed. Yarmouth ME: DeLorme, 2005.

———. *North Dakota Atlas & Gazetteer.* Yarmouth ME: DeLorme, 1999.

———. *South Dakota Atlas & Gazetteer.* 3rd ed. Yarmouth ME: DeLorme, 2004.

———. *Wyoming Atlas & Gazetteer.* 3rd ed. Yarmouth ME: DeLorme, 2001.

Hart, Herbert M. *Tour Guide to Old Western Forts.* Boulder CO: Pruett, 1980.

Jording, Mike. *A Few Interested Residents: Wyoming Historical Markers & Monuments.* Helena MT: SkyHouse, 1992.

Karolevitz, Robert F. *Yankton: A Pioneer Past.* Aberdeen SD: North Plains, 1972.

Koury, Michael J. *Military Posts of Montana.* Bellevue NE: Old Army, 1970.

Leach, Faye. *Historic Markers Monuments and Memorials placed by the Minnesota Daughters of the American Revolution.* Lake Hubert MN: Birchdale, 2015.

Leitch, Barbara. *A Concise Dictionary of Indian Tribes.* Algonac MI: Reference, 1979.

McKusick, Marshall. *The Iowa Northern Border Brigade.* Iowa City: University of Iowa Press, 1975.

Moulton, Candy. *Forts, Fights, and Frontier Sites: Wyoming Historic Sites.* Glendo WY: High Plains, 2010.

Roberts, Robert B. *Encyclopedia of Historic Forts.* New York: McMillan, 1988.

Snortland, J. Signe, ed. *A Traveler's Companion to North Dakota State Historic Sites.* 2nd ed. Bismarck ND: State Historical Society of North Dakota, 2002.

Wyoming Recreation Commission, *Wyoming: A Guide to Historic Sites.* Basin WY: Big Horn, 1976.